ESSENTIAL ELEMENTS

A COMPREHENSIVE BAND METHOD

by

Tom C. Rhodes • Donald Bierschenk • Tim Lautzenheiser • John Higgins

ESSENTIAL ELEMENTS INCLUDES:

Rhythm Raps
• Clapping exercises with percussion accompaniment isolate new rhythms

Essential Elements Quizzes
• Performance quizzes test student's ability on new and review concepts

Theory

• Concise definitions are reinforced with examples

History

• Cultural backgrounds and history of composers appear throughout books
• Histories are related to other significant world events

☆ Sightreading
• Teach the Sightreading guidelines printed in student books
• Watch your band develop into sightreading stars!

Special Highlights
• Multicultural songs add diversity and musical awareness in both books
• Technique Trax exercises develop basic musical skills
• Band arrangements, duets, trios, rounds, section features add to your teaching options
-Also available -

Teacher Resource Kit
• Includes time-saving lesson plans, rhythm dictation, sightreading poster, motivational posters, Music Olympics, and much more
• Complete materials for Book 1 and Book 2 are packaged in one kit

ISBN 0-7935-1285-9

00863536

HAL•LEONARD™
CORPORATION
7777 W. BLUEMOUND RD. P.O. BOX 13819 MILWAUKEE, WI 53213

SEQUENCE OF

Director Page	14-23	24-32	33-41	42-51	52-59	60-66	67-74	75-82	83-91	92-100	101-107	108-112	113-122
Student Page	**2**	**3**	**4**	**5**	**6**	**7**	**8**	**9**	**10**	**11**	**12**	**13**	**14**
Rhythms					¢ or 2/2	♪ 𝄽 𝄽 ♪	♪♪ ♪	♫♫♫		♫♫♫	♫♫	♩. ♪	
Theory				Key Change				Syncopation					
History			Tallis	"Loch Lomond"			Cohan		Elgar			Bizet	Sousa
Terms	Accidentals	Sightreading	Balance **Adagio** Staccato ♩· Tenuto ♩·	*ritardando* **Allegretto**					*rallentando* Legato		Etude	**Maestoso**	
Special Features	Duet Perc. Sticking Methods	Duet *Technique Trax* STARS guidelines *Sightreading Challenge #1*	Chorale for Full Band Round			*mp* *Sightreading Challenge #2*		Duet *Sightreading Challenge #3*	*Technique Trax*		*Sightreading Challenge #4*	Trio	
Quiz Purpose				♩ and ♩ *rit.* Perc. Rudiments			♪♪ ♪ Dynamics Perc. Rudiments		♫ Articulations Dynamics			Maestoso Opera Music	

Note Sequence (instruments, left labels)

- Flute
- Oboe
- Bb Clar.
- Bb Bs. Clar.
- Eb A. Clar.
- Eb A. Sax / Eb B. Sax
- Bb T. Sax
- Bb Tpt. / Bar. T.C.
- F Horn
- Trb. / Bar. B.C. / Bssn.
- Tuba
- Kybd. Perc.

Annotations within staff: alt. (Bb Clar.), alt. (Eb A. Sax), alt. (col.), "(b♮ ♯♮) Tpt. only"

Percussion Rudiments & Techniques

	Double Bounce R R L L / Special Ex.	Guiro	Flamadiddle L R L R R	Double Paradiddle R L R L R R / Bass Drum Roll	¢	Drag L L R / Special Ex.: Added Strokes		Timpani			Triangle Roll	Timpani Roll	

Correlating Band Arrangement Levels: ▲ Artist Level

★ Special Director Pages include **Parent Press Pak** (pgs. 4-11), **Essential Elements Book 2 - Special Features** (pg. 12), **History Of The Band** (pg. 331), **Careers In Music** (pgs. 332-333), **Programming Ideas** (pgs. 334-335), and **Bibliography** (pg. 335) and **Essential Elements Instrumentation** (pg. 336).

ESSENTIAL ELEMENTS

Director Page	123-128	129-139	140-149	150-154	155-163	164-172	173-180	181-187	188-196	197-245	246-257	258-293	294-329	330-336
Student Page	**15**	**16**	**17**	**18**	**19**	**20**	**21**	**22**	**23**	**24-26**	**27**	**28-29**	**30-31**	**32**
Rhythms	6/8			3 (triplet)	(dotted rhythm)									
Theory		Enharmonics, Chromatic Scale									Major Scale			
History		Habañera				"Marines' Hymn"	Waltz, Strauss		Gliére					
Terms				Triplets		D.S. al Fine, accel.		(repeat sign), simile						
Special Features		Technique Trax		Duet		Technique Trax	Duet	Technique Trax		Band Arr.: Simple Gifts, Danny Boy, Semper Fidelis, Take Me Out To The Ballgame, Serengeti	Major Scales, Special Chromatic Scale	Special Exercises for each Instrument	Fingering Charts, 40 Rudiments, Kybd. Perc. Instruments	Glossary, Special* Director Pages
Quiz Purpose	6/8			Sightreading Challenge #5	(rhythm)		(rhythm)							
Note Sequence — Flute														
Oboe														
Bb Clar.														
Bb Bs. Clar.														
Eb A. Clar.														
Eb A. Sax / Eb B. Sax														
Bb T. Sax														
Bb Tpt. / Bar. T.C.												(Bar. only)		
F Horn														
Trb. / Bar. B.C. / Bssn.														
Tuba														
Kybd. Perc.														
Percussion Rudiments & Techniques	Flam Accent, Flam Tap (L R L R L R R)										Special Sticking Exercises			
Correlating Band Arrangement Levels	▲ Expert Level													▲ Master Level

PARENT PRESS PAK

Director Communication with parents is an essential element for a successful band program. The following message and letters provide valuable information for band parents. Fill in the appropriate names and phone numbers, and adapt the written text to meet the individual needs of your program.

DATELINE: Distribute your version of this "Message To Parents" at your first meeting with band parents.

MESSAGE TO PARENTS

A Parent's Guide To Enhancing Your Child's Musical Experiences

CONGRATULATIONS

Your decision to provide your child with a quality musical instrument is an investment in your child's future. In making it possible for your child to play a musical instrument, you are providing the opportunity for self-expression, creativity and achievement.

Numerous studies indicate that parental attitude, support and involvement are important factors in a child's ability to successfully learn to play and to enjoy music.

These guidelines are designed to assist you in giving your child the best support possible for his or her musical endeavors. Like any skill, interest counts far more than talent. With the right support from you, playing music will become a natural part of your child's life.

BENEFITS

For Your Child

Music participation enhances:
- Problem solving
- Teamwork
- Goal setting
- Self-expression
- Coordination
- Memory skills
- Self-confidence and esteem
- Concentration
- Poise
- and much, much more!

For Your Family

A child's music study also offers opportunities for shared family experiences including:
- Musical event attendance
- Family music-making
- Performing for, and with, family and friends
- Learning about the lives of composers and the cultural heritage of many civilizations
- A sense of accomplishment and pride for the entire family

HOW YOU FIT IN

Always keep in mind that your support is an essential element in your child's success with music study.

Schedule Practice Times

Music achievement requires effort over a period of time. You can help your child by:
- Providing a quiet place in which to practice.
- Remaining nearby during practice times as often as possible.
- Scheduling a consistent, daily time for practice.
- Praising your child's efforts and achievements.

Selecting A Music Teacher

Formal music instruction can help your child's progress. In choosing a teacher, consider these points:
- Background and experience
- Comments from other parents and students
- Provisions for sharing music through performance

As your child's band director, I can recommend excellent private teacher(s) in our community. You may also wish to contact (local music dealer) who will provide you with a list of qualified instructors. For a list of nationally certified private teachers, contact the Music Teachers National Association (see "Credits" section).

WHAT TO DO

To give your child the best possible support, you should:
- Encourage your child to play for family and friends.
- Offer compliments and encouragement regularly.
- Expose your child to a wide variety of music, including concerts and recitals.
- Encourage your child to talk with you about his or her lessons.
- Make sure your child's instrument is always in good working order.
- Allow your child to play many types of music, not just study pieces.
- Listen to your child practice, and acknowledge improvement.
- Help your child build a personal music library.
- Try to get your child to make a minimum two-year commitment to his or her music studies.

WHAT NOT TO DO

Your child's progress will be greatly enhanced if you...
- Don't use practice as a punishment.
- Don't insist your child play for others when they don't want to.
- Don't ridicule or make fun of mistakes or less-than-perfect playing.
- Don't apologize to others for your child's weak performance.
- Don't start your child on an instrument that's in poor working order or condition.
- Don't expect rapid progress and development in the beginning.

IF YOUR CHILD LOSES INTEREST

In the event that your child loses interest in his or her music studies, don't panic.
- Discuss the situation with your child to determine why their interest is declining.
- Talk to your child's music teacher to see what might be done to rekindle their enthusiasm.
- Encourage your child to stick with lessons for an agreed to period of time.
- Offer increased enthusiasm and support.

CREDITS

This message has been developed by the following organizations in the interest of making music study and participation an enjoyable and richly rewarding experience for children and their families. Hal Leonard Publishing Corporation appreciates the cooperation of these organizations for graciously allowing us to reprint this message.

AMERICAN MUSIC CONFERENCE
303 East Wacker Drive, Suite 1214
Chicago, IL 60601
(312) 856-8820

MUSIC EDUCATORS NATIONAL CONFERENCE
1902 Association Drive
Reston, VA 22091
(703) 860-4000

MUSIC TEACHERS NATIONAL ASSOCIATION
617 Vine St., Suite 1432
Cincinnati, OH 45202-2434
(513) 421-1420

NATIONAL ASSOCIATION OF MUSIC MERCHANTS
5140 Avenida Encinas
Carlsbad, CA 92008-4391
(619) 438-8001

DATELINE: Send within one week of child's start in **Essential Elements Book 2**.

Dear Band Parent/s,

We enthusiastically welcome you to **Essential Elements, Book 2**. CONGRATULATIONS are extended to your (son/daughter) for completing the requirements and mastering the skills and techniques offered in **Book 1**. Band will now take on another level of enjoyment and challenge as (name of student) enters the next realm in (his/her) musical career.

It was only a few months ago that the band was learning to put their instruments together and working to produce a representative sound. We are now successfully reading music, exchanging solos, preparing for upcoming concerts, and realizing the benefits of several months of committed practice. Thank you for your support during the crucial introduction period. You have served as a valuable partner in this fundamental learning process.

Essential Elements, Book 1 serves as an important prelude to the artistic excitement of **Book 2**. Although the journey to excellence is a life-long quest, the basics are now a part of your child's musical vocabulary. This next phase requires a more disciplined focus and a continued dedication to individual practice and attention to detail. As you quickly ascertain, *YOU* play a vital role in this endeavor. The habits which are encouraged and supported from your vantage point will be a vital factor in the ongoing success of (name of child)'s growth and development. Let us move forward together in mutual harmony. *You* are an "essential element" in this certain formula for success.

Thank you for your time, energy, and ongoing support of our band. Any communication which concerns the welfare of the program and/or your young musician is encouraged. Once again, we welcome you to a new stage of performance as we continue to *Strike Up The Band!*

Musically yours,

Band Director

DATELINE: Send 3-6 weeks into the **Essential Elements Book 2** program.

Dear Band Parent/s,

It is time to share a *Positive Progress Report* with you about the ongoing success of our band program and the important contribution that (name of student) is making to the ensemble. You must be very proud of (his/her)'s continued mastery of the instrument.

The language of music knows no boundaries. It has the ability to transcend every man-made barrier and express the inner soul of the human. In the formative years of band, we often overlook this extraordinary communication potential. It is easy to get caught up in the technical calisthenics and lose sight of the real purpose in choosing the study of music. As new demands are made on the performer, it is important for all of us to remind the young musician there is an important life prospering aesthetic reason for the effort.

A high level of proficiency creates a higher expectancy from each member of the organization. The goals of the band are now more advanced and thus the attainment of these objectives requires a greater sense of commitment from every member. Your encouragement is a key factor in this quest. Persistence is an *essential element*. Establishing daily practice habits will ensure personal triumph for your child. Let us join together in accomplishing this end on (his/her) behalf.

As always, you are encouraged to share your thoughts and feelings concerning the progress of (name of child) and the growth of the (name of school) band. Thank you for "banding together" with us in this meaningful learning experience for all of the students. We will look forward to having you with us at our next public concert, (date, time, etc.)

Musically yours,

Band Director

DATELINE: Send 3-4 months into the **Essential Elements Book 2** program.

Dear Band Parent/s,

Many have said the *benefits of band* extend far beyond the mastery and understanding of musical technique. The nurturing of a positive self-image is a certain reward for any student who plays an active roll in the band community. Ongoing research confirms that *students of music* score higher in academic subjects and are actively sought by colleges and universities not only for their musical talents, but because they rank at the top of their classes in school. Let us spotlight this hidden advantage for your understanding of the positive implications band plays in the future of your (son/daughter).

Ultimately, we are developing young people to be successful at anything they choose to do in life. The study of music enhances every aspect of their future. It affords them the opportunity to reach into their personal potential and enjoy the achievement of both personal and group goals. Author Robert C. Hawley stated in his book, Human Values in the Classroom,

> *"Over time, a continuing and steadfast focus on the positive in life, on our strengths, and on the strengths of others can help to restore in our students their personal energy, their feelings of importance, their sense of self-worth so they can see themselves as positive forces who can contribute to the task of building a better world."*

This is one of the major themes which serves as a basic component of every band practice. It is important that each member feel positive about his/her participation and they see themselves as an integral contributor to the overall success of the entire program. Everyone *is* important! Everyone has worth. Everyone makes a difference in our band.

Thank you for your time. I would be delighted to visit with you about the progress of (name of student). Our next concert is (time, date, etc.).

In the interest of your child,

Band Director

DATELINE: Send 2 weeks prior to concert.

Dear Band Parent/s,

It seems as if only yesterday you were sent a "welcome to beginning band" letter, and now you are a veteran band parent with many wonderful musical experiences to share with your family and friends. Thank you for your much appreciated support. You have played an integral role in the success of the (name of school) band program.

(Name of child) has been one of the key members of the band and is well deserving of your acknowledgment and praise. These purposeful musicians who have made the extra effort are now enjoying the fruits of their labor as we move into the next domain of musical expression. This degree of commitment and follow-through will be evident in every successful aspect of their lives.

The (name of school) band would like to honor all the parents in a special *THANK YOU CONCERT* scheduled for (date, time, etc.). As you well know, the most important audience in the world is Mom and Dad. This is an opportunity for all the talented band students to musically express their appreciation for your continued support and encouragement. Please be with us for this very important event.

It has been my distinct pleasure to work with all of the aspiring young musicians for I know their investment will bring benefits to every avenue of their life. Whether it is via participation in a community band, playing in the church orchestra, or seeking music as a profession, every student's future is certain to be embellished because of MUSIC. Yes, there was much technical information exchanged in the study of the *essential elements,* however the real learning was the process of self-discovery.

Join us in this special celebration. We *strike up the band* on your behalf and in your honor.

With appreciation

Band Director

DATELINE: A letter for parents about home practice.

Dear Band Parent/s,

The excitement of a new adventure is enough to provide an ample supply of positive motivation for the first months of the band experience. Once the initial enthusiasm wears off, it is important to immediately develop wholesome practice habits which will guarantee a successful and personally gratifying learning process for your child. Your support and guidance *will be* the key factors in establishing the practice schedule insuring the attainment of the musical goals.

The most effective home rehearsal programs are based on a daily half hour dedicated to quality practice. It is suggested that you and your young musicians mutually agree on a practice time, and a special area of your home which is designated as their area of musical study. Every effort should be made to establish a disciplined pattern which is encouraged and acknowledged by you. A final five to ten minute recital of the new material is always effective in building performance responsibilities. Every instrumentalist enjoys the opportunity to display his/her talents. You might even ask for a paragraph of what new progress was made during practice. A special calendar can also serve as a reminder as well as a reward poster for the commitment needed to accomplish the assigned material. Remember, positive reinforcement is the most effective communication you can share in this important quest.

It is vital to develop a discipline which makes home practice a natural part of the day. Although many of the new concepts will be taught during band rehearsals, the limited time does not afford the personal attention which is vital in developing technical facility required for the upcoming years of musical exploration. The cooperative efforts of the band director, the student musician, and the willing parents constitute the proven recipe of success.

Band means more to your child than just playing an instrument. It offers an opportunity to experience a new level of communication. This artistic language will be with them for a lifetime. These formative years of music education can open up a world of aesthetic possibilities which will bring new meaning to the growth and development of your child. Let us join hands in establishing a solid foundation of growth by creating a disciplined practice schedule early in their musical career.

Your thoughts and questions are encouraged.

Musically yours,

Band Director

DATELINE: Send when a child is thinking about quitting band.

Dear (name of parent/s),   (BE PERSONAL!)

I have learned that (name of child) is thinking about ending (his/her) participation in band. This is an important decision that could have an impact on the future of (his/her) academic career as well as affect (his/her) appreciation of all facets of life. Though it may seem like a very small decision based on the short amount of time invested so far in the process of learning a musical instrument, I encourage you to spend a few minutes mutually going over some important information that may not be familiar to you. Can you afford not to?

(Name of parent/s), I certainly do not want to infringe on your right as a parent to support your (son/daughter)'s decision, but would ask that we might discuss this matter. I would like for you to have the opportunity to help (name of child) make this choice with a complete awareness of the investment to date, the benefits which are forthcoming, the future of (his/her) role in the program, and how important the habit of persistence is in every avenue of life.

M.A. Rees, in an open letter to band parents in one of our most respected instrumental publications stated, "Successful music students tend to possess the qualities and skills that are considered essential to employers in business, education, and service organizations. They are ahead of others in writing, communication skills, and analytical skills. They also have a high degree of self discipline." Isn't this what we all want for our young people?

(Name of child) is going through the formative years of habit-development. These habits will determine the way (he/she) approaches every aspect of life. Though the requirements for learning an instrument often demand a high level of personal discipline; it is this discipline which will be applied as a habit to all tasks in life. (Name of child) deserves the best. Herein lies a way to see that this is established.

Please contact me at your earliest convenience and let's have a conversation that will allow you to help (name of child) make the best decision possible for (his/her) future. Rest assured, I will support whatever choice is made. However, let's make sure that it is based on solid information for we are dealing with society's most important investment: tomorrow's leaders.

THANK YOU FOR YOUR TIME AND PERSONAL ATTENTION.

Musically yours,

The Band Director

ESSENTIAL ELEMENTS BOOK 2 — SPECIAL FEATURES

ABOUT THE BAND ARRANGEMENTS IN THIS BOOK . . .

As you take your students through this second book of **Essential Elements**, you may wish to gradually start introducing your students to the full band arrangements which appear at the end of this book. Having completed the first book of **Essential Elements**, your students already possess many of the skills needed to start rehearsing these arrangements.

We encourage you to work on one or several of these arrangements each day with your students as part of their regular lesson. Not only will your students enjoy the challenge of these full band arrangements, but by the time your students have completed **Essential Elements** Book 2, they will also be prepared to present these pieces in a full concert.

The full band arrangements included in **Essential Elements** Book 2 are:

> *118. Simple Gifts*
> *119. Danny Boy*
> *120. Semper Fidelis*
> *121. Take Me Out To The Ballgame*
> *122. Serengeti (An African Rhapsody)*

These pieces have been carefully selected and arranged to offer a well-balanced concert program which combines all of the essential elements learned throughout the course. Complete Rehearsal Guides for all **Essential Elements** band arrangements are included in the **Teacher Resource Kit** (available separately).

ABOUT THE SPECIAL INSTRUMENT PAGES IN THIS BOOK . . .

Pages 28 and 29 of each student book contain special exercises designed to isolate problems and techniques specific to each individual instrument. These pages are not intended to be used in the full band setting, but rather as supplementary material used to augment the student's regular daily lesson. These pages contain exercises that will benefit all students at any level of ability. Tempos are left up to the director and student to decide, depending on the student's ability. Advanced students should be encouraged to practice these pages regularly, constantly working to increase the tempos to improve their abilities and techniques. Students needing additional help can work on specific exercises which isolate their difficulty at their own speed until they can master the skill with confidence.

ABOUT THE PERCUSSION BOOK . . .

Proper sticking for percussionists is like proper fingerings for the various instruments in the band. Various methods of sticking are used in percussion music today. In early percussion music, most parts were written in the rudimental style based on the patterns used by the military snare drummers on parade. These rudimental patterns are still valuable exercises today, used to develop strength and dexterity. Alternating, or hand-to-hand sticking, demands that the performer switch hands on every note, thus developing the right and left hands equally. With the emphasis and focus on today's percussionist in much of our contemporary literature, the adaptation of Right Hand Lead sticking has become a preference for many professional percussionists, for it is consistent and transferable to all the instruments in the percussion family.

Essential Elements recognizes all three of the sticking methods as an important and essential part of every fine percussionist's technical abilities. They each represent a vital part of the skill development. We do suggest, however, that for accurate reading ability, your students develop a solid understanding of Right Hand Lead. All Right Hand Lead exercises are indicated with a *. (In **Essential Elements** Book 1, we called this "Superstar Sticking".)

Dear Band Student,

CONGRATULATIONS! You have graduated to the next level of your band experience and are ready to enjoy a new beginning of exciting benefits designed for you and your fellow musicians.

Have you noticed how much better you are playing, counting, listening, and enjoying band? The many hours of quality practice are opening up new opportunities for everyone in your group. You are ready to move to the next level of challenging musical benefits, and they await you in the following pages.

There are so many extra rewards band people enjoy: working together in harmony, performing for parents and friends, having a family of fellow musicians, being recognized by others as a talented person, enjoying a high degree of personal accomplishment, and a treasury of other positive feelings and experiences. You are taking advantage of the chance of a lifetime. Music is the language of the world.

Most importantly, you have chosen to be a part of an organization which has been a proving ground for many of today's most successful people. Your achievements and accomplishments in band are guiding you towards excellence in every part of your life.

We welcome you to Essential Elements Book 2 with the well wishes for continued success on your musical journey. *Strike Up The Band!*

Percussion: Sticking Methods   Several methods of sticking are used when playing the snare drum. These include Alternate Sticking (R L R L), Single Hand Sticking (R R R R or L L L L), Right Hand Lead (R on strong divisions of the beat), and Rudimental Sticking (uses basic rudiments). You will see several sticking methods indicated throughout this book. Right Hand Lead exercises are labeled with a ✱, Alternate Sticking exercises are labeled with A, and wrist builder exercises using Single Hand Sticking are labeled WB. Rudimental exerises show the name of the rudiment the first time it appears above the sticking like this:

Paradiddle
R   L   R   R

When no sticking is indicated, follow your director's instructions on which sticking method to use.

Director   *1. Harmonized Concert B♭ Scale* can be used as a warm-up exercise to begin each rehearsal. You may wish to have your students play this exercise in a variety of ways — adding different styles, articulations and dynamics — either verbally indicated to your students before they begin or conveyed through your conducting style. Always encourage your students to listen to each other as they play. Warm up slowly and point out the various harmonic intervals. Stress the importance of intonation.

Students will also enjoy performing full band arrangements from the **Essential Elements Band Series — Artist Level**. These concert selections reinforce all material introduced throughout **Essential Elements** Book 1. Each student part includes an "Essential Elements" page of valuable learning exercises. Call your favorite band music dealer for more information.

Percussion: Listen to the harmony played by the band.

1. HARMONIZED CONCERT B♭ SCALE (What is the scale name for your instrument?)

NEW NOTES INTRODUCED ON 2. THE ASH GROVE
Concert B♭

Oboe

Director Several concepts are reviewed in *2. The Ash Grove* which were developed in **Essential Elements** Book 1 such as Andante, ¾ meter, pick-up note, slurs, and repeat sign. Briefly review these concepts with your students before playing.

---

2. THE ASH GROVE

Old Welsh Air

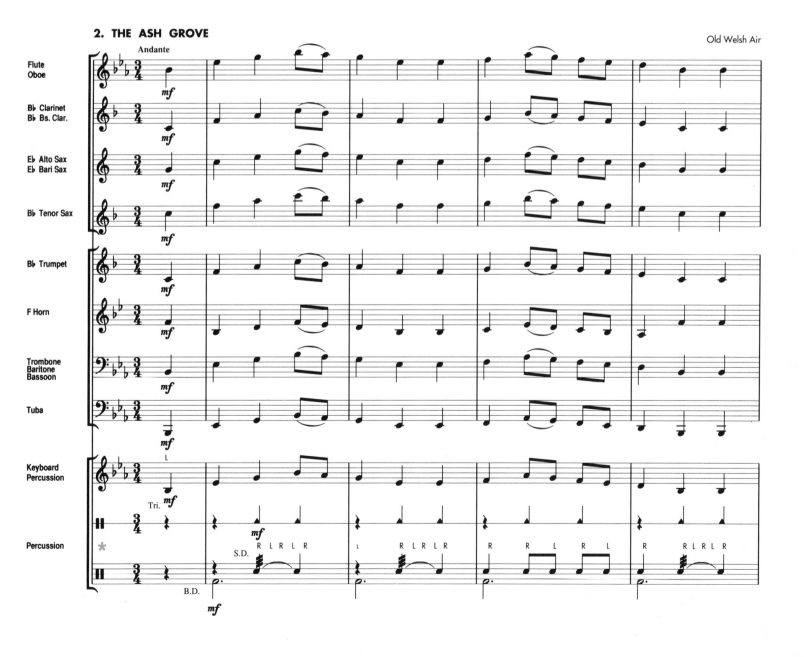

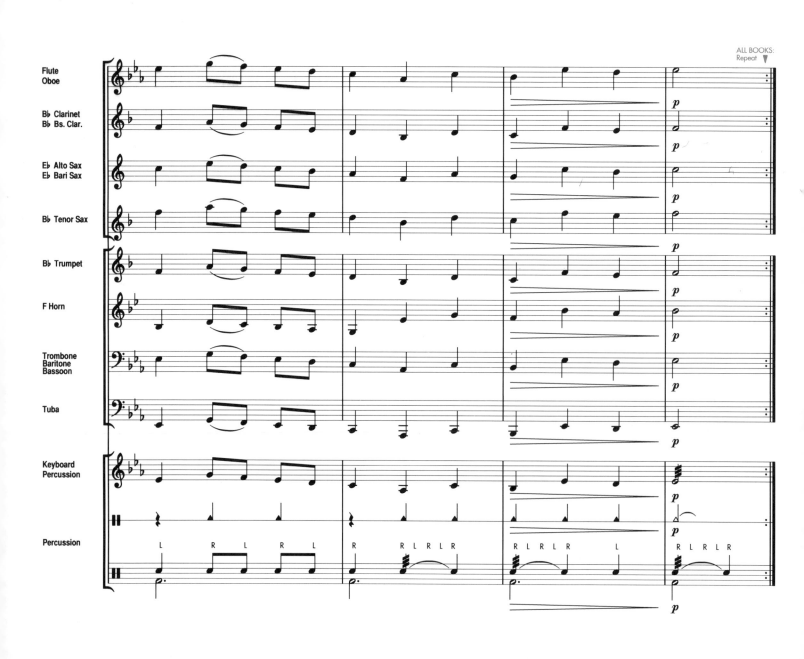

Director This counting exercise concentrates on simple meter changes between ¾ and 𝄴 time. Have your students count, clap and tap before playing. After learning this exercise you may want to divide the class and have one group conduct while the other group plays the exercise. Review the basic conducting patterns learned in Book 1.

Percussion: **Snares Off** Playing with the snares off produces a hollow tom-tom sound on the snare drum. Another time to turn the snares off is when the drums are NOT playing. This prevents the snares from vibrating and making rattling sounds while the rest of the band is playing. This is especially helpful when the band is playing very softly.

Director Review the dotted quarter note rhythm used in *4. Song of Kites* with your students.

4. SONG OF KITES

Japanese Children's Song

Percussion: Double Bounce  A double bounce is a controlled multiple bounce consisting of only two bounces per stroke. Rolls that use double bounces are called open rolls. Begin practicing the following exercise at slow tempos gradually increasing speed to develop smooth double bounce rolls.

Director Although we advocate the multiple bounce or closed roll method of teaching rolls in the beginning stages, you may wish to have your percussionists play double bounce or open rolls as their technique becomes more advanced.

NEW NOTES INTRODUCED ON 5. CHROMATIC CRUISE

Concert A

Oboe

A

Accidentals Sharps (♯), flats (♭), or naturals (♮) found in the music but not in the key signature.
Percussion: It is very important that you watch for accidentals when you are playing keyboard percussion instruments.

Director Give your students a few minutes to silently finger through this exercise on their own before playing. Encourage them to look for and solve potential fingering problems BEFORE they begin playing.

5. CHROMATIC CRUISE

Director   Through **Essential Elements**, you will find several *Technique Trax* exercises. These exercises drill basic musical technique which will help your students to gain more facility on their instrument. Students should be encouraged to practice these exercises on their own striving for the fastest possible tempo, but still maintaining complete *accuracy*. Teach your students how to correctly practice these exercises, always beginning slowly and taking care not to get faster until the exercise is mastered at the slow tempo.

Percussionists usually have *Wrist Builder* sticking indications on all *Technique Trax* exercises. Make sure your percussionists follow these stickings in order to help build equal wrist technique and control in both hands. Encourage them to watch their stick height to make sure both hands are working equally.

Percussion: Use the indicated sticking to help build strength in both wrists.

6. TECHNIQUE TRAX   Practice slowly at first, then gradually increase your tempo.

Director   Practice lines A and B separately in *7. Salsa Siesta* . Then divide your class and play as a duet. Insist that everyone play the dynamics accurately. The use of the traditional Latin American percussion instruments make this a fun exercise for your percussionists. You may need to review the correct playing technique for maracas and claves. (This part is found in the keyboard percussion book.) After your class can play this duet with confidence, you may wish to pass around the Latin American percussion instruments to various members of the class and encourage them to make up their own special percussion parts to fit with the band.

Percussion: Guiro   The guiro (pronounced *we' ro*) is a Latin American instrument usually in the shape of a gourd with hollowed-out notches on the side. It is played by scraping a stick along the notched side. A good sound will result if you keep constant pressure on the stick while scraping.

7. SALSA SIESTA - Duet   Play all dynamics carefully!

Director   Be certain students count, clap and tap all exercises before playing them. Begin by counting, clapping and tapping
slowly with your students. Then ask them to demonstrate these skills without your help.

8. RHYTHM ON THE RANGE   Count and clap before playing.

Sightreading   Playing a musical selection for the first time. The key to sightreading success is to know what to look for before playing the piece. Follow the guidelines below, and your band will be sightreading STARS! Use the word **STARS** to remind yourself what to look for before reading a selection the first time.

S — **Sharps or flats** in the **key signature**   Identify the key signature first. Silently practice notes from the key signature. Look for key signature changes in the piece.

T — **Time signature** and **tempo markings**   Identify and look for changes in the piece.

A — **Accidentals**   Check for any accidentals not found in the key signature.

R — **Rhythm**   Slowly count and clap all difficult rhythms. Pay special attention to rests.

S — **Signs**   Look for all signs that indicate dynamics, articulations, tempo changes, repeats, 1st and 2nd endings, and any other instructions printed on your music.

Percussion and Keyboard Percussion: Percussionists should check the music carefully to make sure all instruments and mallets are ready before beginning to play.

Director   *Sightreading Challenges* provide you and your students the opportunity to work on this important skill as a class. Frequently drill the **STARS** acronym with your students, and encourage them to memorize it. (A shorter version of it appears on *33. Sightreading Challenge #2.*) Discuss each element of sightreading as it specifically pertains to each exercise. A large colorful sightreading poster highlighting the **STARS** acronym is included in the **Teacher Resource Kit.**

9. SIGHTREADING CHALLENGE #1

Balance   The proper adjustment of volume and sound from all the instruments in the band playing together. Good balance is achieved when each section of the band can be heard equally. While playing *Balance Builder* listen carefully and follow your director's instructions to make sure your sound blends with the rest of the band.

Percussion: The proper adjustment of volume and sound from all the instruments in the band playing together. Good balance is achieved when each section of the band can be heard equally. Percussionists should listen carefully to make sure you can always hear the band parts while you play. While playing *Balance Builder* listen carefully and follow your director's instructions to make sure your sound blends with the rest of the band.

Percussion: Flamadiddle  A snare drum rudiment.

Director   *10. Balance Builder - Chorale* is arranged for full band. Rehearse each section individually, giving the rest of the band an opportunity to listen to each voice before it is played together. As your class plays together, remind them to listen carefully for each section and remind them to watch you for balance indications.

You will probably want to play this exercise both with and without percussion. Although the winds will be able to listen better without the drums playing, you need to teach your percussionists to make their sound blend with the rest of the band also. Remind your percussionists to follow the indicated flamadiddle stickings.

10. BALANCE BUILDER - Chorale

English composer **Thomas Tallis** (1505-1585) served as a royal court composer during the reigns of Henry VIII, Edward VI, Mary and Elizabeth. The great artist, Michaelangelo, painted the Sistine Chapel during Tallis' lifetime. Canons and rounds were among the popular types of 16th century forms of music that Tallis wrote. Divide into groups and play *Tallis Canon* as a four-part round.

Director Review with your students the idea of the canon or round as a simple form of *counterpoint.* You may want to further explore the music of the Renaissance with your students by playing various recorded examples for them.

Divide your class into parts and review with them how to play a round:

1st group starts at 1 and plays to the end.
2nd group starts at 1 when the first group reaches 2 and plays to the end.
3rd group starts at 1 when the first group reaches 3 and plays to the end.
4th group starts at 1 when the first group reaches 4 and plays to the end.

This particular round is slightly more challenging since all entrances begin on beat four rather than beat one. You may want to begin practicing with only two groups until your students develop confidence in their entrances.

11. TALLIS CANON - Round

Thomas Tallis

NEW NOTES INTRODUCED ON 12. STACCATO STEAMBOAT
Concert G
Concert B♭ (Horn)

Staccato 𝅘𝅥 or 𝅘𝅥 Staccato notes are marked with a dot above or below the note. Play these notes lightly and with separation.
Percussion: Staccato notes are marked with a dot above or below the note. Play these notes lightly and with separation. Producing staccato on percussion is different on each instrument. On the snare drum the sound is already separated because of the nature of the instrument, while the bass drum or triangle must be muffled (choked) immediately to produce a staccato effect.

Try the next exercise using any percussion instrument. Experiment with different methods to produce the most staccato sound possible on that instrument.
Keyboard Percussion: Staccato notes are marked with a dot above or below the note. Play these notes lightly and with separation. Try to imitate the sounds made by the winds. To play staccato, snap your wrist a little faster.

Director Remind your students to maintain full breath support when playing staccato notes. Be sure they end the notes by stopping the air — not by using the tongue which creates a very heavy "tut" sound.

Remind your Horn players to use the "T" fingering on the final note if they are playing a double horn.

12. STACCATO STEAMBOAT

13. PAT - A - PAN

Bernard de la Monnoye

Tenuto ♩ or ⏜ Tenuto notes are marked with a straight line above or below the note. Play these notes smooth and connected, holding each note for its full value.

Keyboard Percussion: Tenuto notes are marked with a straight line above or below the note. Play these notes smooth and connected, without any break. Let the tones ring together.

Percussion: Tenuto notes are marked with a straight line above or below the note. Play these notes smooth and connected, holding each note for its full value. On percussion instruments this mark would indicate to let the notes ring for their full duration before muffling or dampening. This pertains to instruments such as timpani, keyboard percussion, triangle, suspended cymbal, crash cymbal, and bass drum.

Director You may wish to have your students use a "du" syllable when playing tenuto notes.

14. TENUTO TIME

NEW NOTES INTRODUCED ON 15. GLOW WORM
Concert G♯
Concert A (Alto Sax, Bari Sax)

Percussion: Bass Drum Roll When rolling on the bass drum, use two bass drum mallets of equal size and roll on the same side of the drum, playing on opposite ends of the bass drum head for best resonance.

Ritardando *(ritard.) (rit.)* Gradually slow the tempo.

15. GLOW WORM

Paul Lincke

NEW NOTES INTRODUCED ON 16. LOCH LOMOND
Concert D

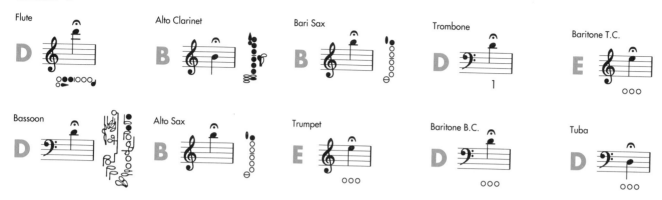

History — Many famous folk songs are about geographical places. The Scottish folk song *Loch Lomond* is one such folk song. Loch (Lake) Lomond is a lake of Scotland renowned for its breathtaking beauty. Located in the southern highlands, it is almost entirely surrounded by hills. One of these is Ben Lomond, a peak 3,192 feet high.

Director — Ask your students to come up with a list of songs written about geographical places. You may want to coordinate a project with the history or geography teacher and have your students locate these places on a map. Have a contest for your students to try to find songs from as many areas of the world as they can.

16. LOCH LOMOND

Scottish Folk Song

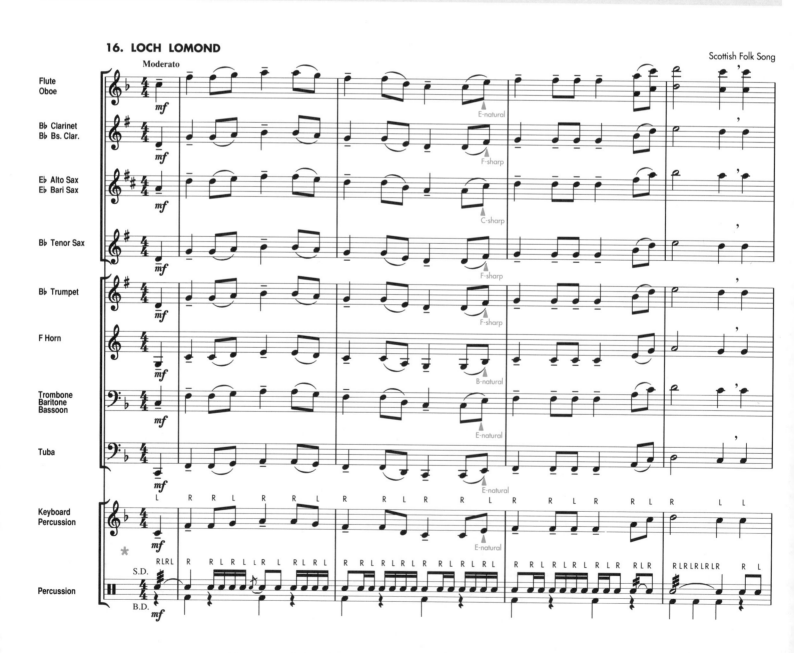

 **Key Change**
Sometimes a key signature will change in the middle of a piece of music. You will usually see a thin double bar line at a key change. Keep going, making sure you are playing all the correct notes in the new signature.

Percussion: When you see this double bar line in a percussion part, listen closely to the band to see if you can hear the change in key.

Percussion: Double Paradiddle
R L R L R R L R L R L L   A snare drum rudiment.

Percussion: Find all Double Paradiddles in this exercise.

Director Remind your students to study both the first key signature and the key signature change BEFORE they play 17. *A Change of Key.* Percussionists should use the double paradiddle stickings as indicated.

17. A CHANGE OF KEY

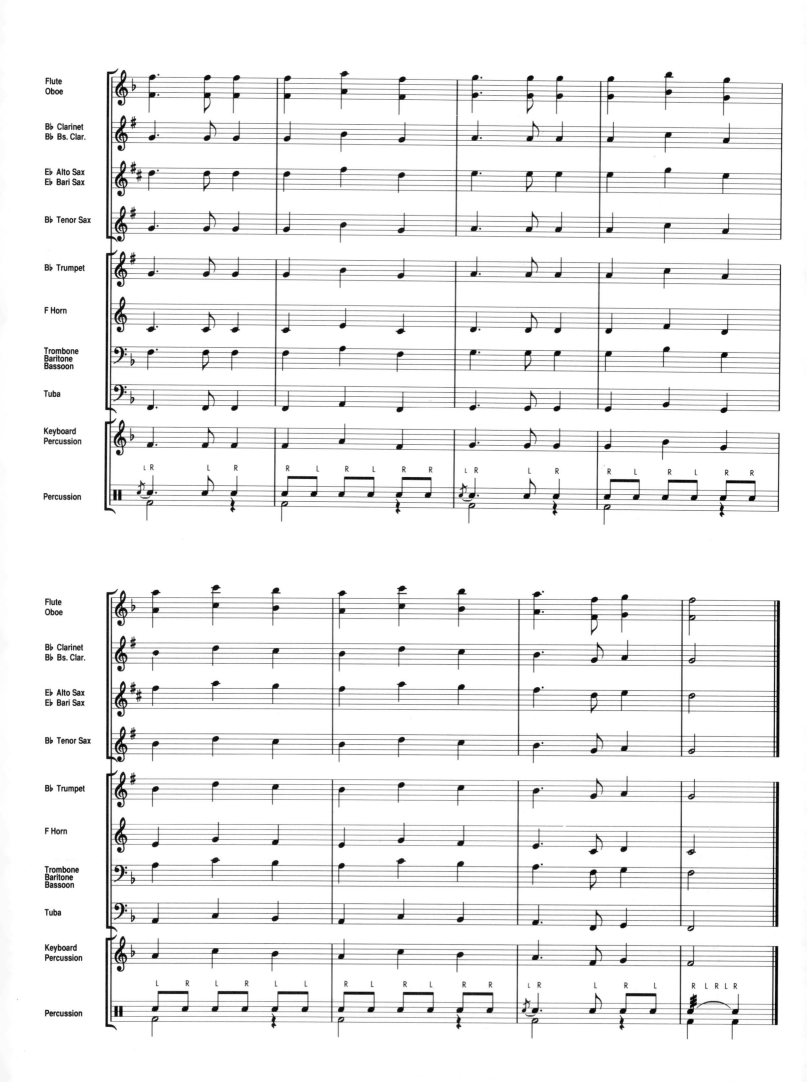

Director Point out the contrasting styles of staccato notes (light and separated) and tenuto notes (smooth, connected, full value). Make certain students are using correct tonguing on sixteenth notes, not using a "breath tongue".

18. CONTRASTS IN B♭ CONCERT

Director The Objectives for each *Essential Elements Quiz* are listed throughout both Director books. The Purpose column highlights the exact elements being tested and reviewed on each quiz. Review Skills suggest specific exercises for students requiring additional practice. Closure Questions and other evaluation criteria are found on the Lesson Plans in the **Teacher Resource Kit.** Be certain students meet your performance expectations on every *Essential Elements Quiz.*

OBJECTIVES FOR 19. ESSENTIAL ELEMENTS QUIZ

Purpose: **Staccato and Tenuto articulations**
Ritardando (rit.)
Percussion: Rudiment
                Identification

Review Exercises: **12. Staccato Steamboat**
13. Pat-A-Pan
14. Tenuto Time
15. Glow Worm
18. Contrasts in B♭ Concert

Percussion: Name all rudiments used in this exercise.

Time Signature (Meter) **Cut Time (Alla Breve)**

¢ or **2/2** - 2 beats per measure
2/2 - ♩ or — gets one beat

o	= 2 beats
♩	= 1 beat
♩	= 1/2 beat
Percussion:	
♪	= 1/4 beat

Special Percussion Exercise

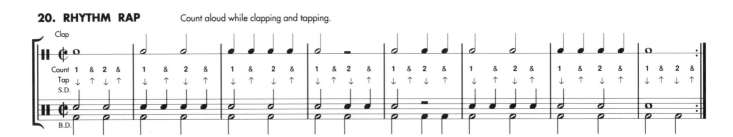

Director *Rhythm Raps* introduce new rhythms and meters to the band. The Percussion book includes the single clapping line plus an accompaniment. Follow this four-step teaching sequence:
• Count, clap and tap the single line until everyone demonstrates it to your satisfaction. Be certain percussionists clap the single line in unison with the band.
• Add the percussion accompaniment while the rest of the band claps the single line. Students count aloud while clapping.
• Clap the line as a round, with and without percussion accompaniment.
• Sing the *Rhythm Rap* on "tah" with percussion accompaniment.

20. RHYTHM RAP   Count aloud while clapping and tapping.

Director Percussionists perform eighth notes in cut time on this exercise. Review the *Special Percussion Exercise* above *20. Rhythm Rap* before counting and clapping this exercise with the entire band.

21. A CUT ABOVE

Director Exercises *22. Two-Four Doodle* and *23. Cut-Time Doodle* demonstrate the same familiar melody written two ways. Point out to your students that even though these two exercises look very different, they should sound exactly the same.

22. TWO - FOUR DOODLE

Percussion: Rolls in Cut Time   When playing in cut time, the hand motion for the roll is the same as the counts. For example:

23. CUT - TIME DOODLE

24. MARIANNE

Jamaican Folk Song

Director Be certain to count and clap *25. The Victors March* before playing. Pay special attention to the new rhythm of dotted half-quarter found in measures 10 and 18.

25. THE VICTORS MARCH

NEW NOTES INTRODUCED ON 26. GOOD KING WENCESLAS
Concert C

26. GOOD KING WENCESLAS

English Carol

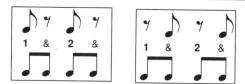

Eighth Rest   𝄾 = 1/2 beat rest

Director   This *Rhythm Rap* isolates eighth notes followed by eighth rests. Point out to your students that the percussion plays on the band's rests.

Rhythm Rap teaching sequence: Entire band claps • Add percussion accompaniment • Clap as a round • Sing on "tah".

Director   The rhythms of *27. Rhythm Rap* and *28. Eighth Notes on the Beat* are identical. Be sure to count, clap and tap all exercises before playing them. Point out that staccato quarter notes and the eighth note-eighth rest patterns look different, but should sound the same.

28. EIGHTH NOTES ON THE BEAT

Percussion: Drag  A snare drum rudiment consisting of a double bounce and a single stroke.

29. A - ROVING

Percussion: Added Strokes — The method in which the snare drum produces notes which sound longer is through the use of adding additional notes to the primary stroke. Listen to the length of the note change as you play the following exercise on snare drum.

Special Percussion Exercise

(Single stroke)   (Flam)   (Drag)   (5 stroke roll)

Director — This *Rhythm Rap* isolates eighth rests off the beat. Point out to your students that the percussion plays on the band's rests.

Rhythm Rap teaching sequence: Entire band claps • Add percussion accompaniment • Clap as a round • Sing on "tah"

30. RHYTHM RAP

Director — The rhythms of *30. Rhythm Rap* and *31. Eighth Notes off the Beat* are identical.

31. EIGHTH NOTES OFF THE BEAT

32. EIGHTH NOTE HOP

Review the **STARS** guidelines before sightreading.

S — Sharps or flats in the key signature
T — Time signature and tempos
A — Accidentals
R — Rhythm
S — Signs

Percussion: Percussionists should check the music carefully to make sure all instruments and mallets are ready before beginning to play.

Director   Review the **STARS** guidelines with your students, and encourage memorization of this acronym. Discuss each element of **STARS** as it pertains to the following exercise.

33. SIGHTREADING CHALLENGE #2

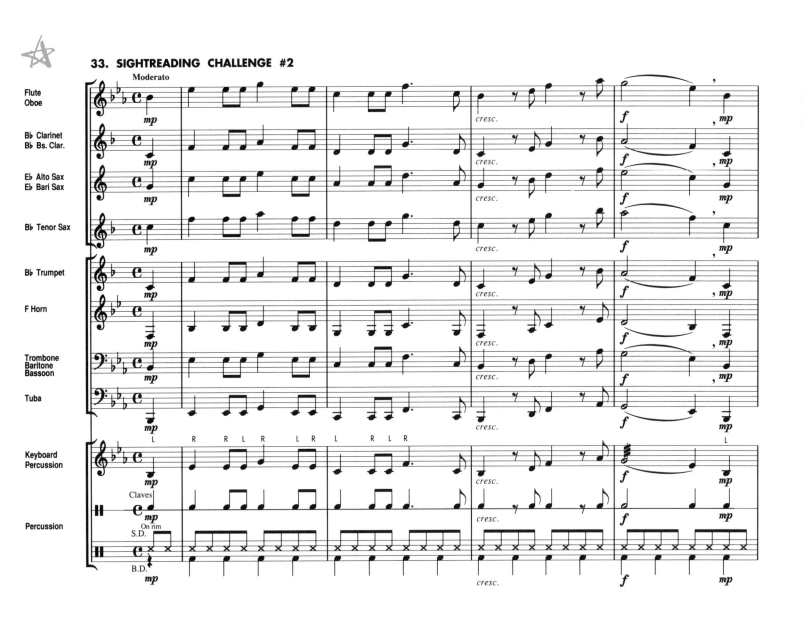

NEW NOTES INTRODUCED ON 34. CONCERT C SCALE EXCERCISE
Concert B

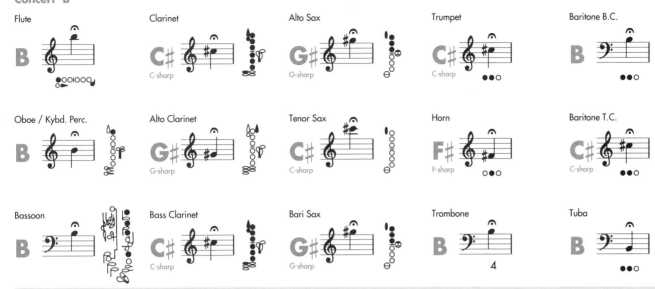

Director The individual instrument scale name appears in all student books next to the title of *34. Concert C Scale Exercise.* Your students should begin to memorize both the Concert scale name and the scale name for their own instrument.

C Instruments: (Your C Scale)
B♭ Instruments: (Your D Scale)
E♭ Instruments: (Your A Scale)
F Instruments: (Your G Scale)
Percussion: Play this exercise as a wrist builder, playing the entire exercise with your left hand.

34. CONCERT C SCALE EXCERCISE

Director Remind students to check the key signature carefully before beginning to play. Insist on accurate articulations throughout.

35. THE MINSTREL BOY

Irish Folk Song

Theory · Syncopation · In many types of music, the accent or emphasis occurs on notes that do not normally receive a strong pulse or beat. This is called **syncopation** and is very common in jazz, rock and pop, as well as in classical music.

Director · When playing syncopated rhythms, it is very important for your students to always be thinking of the eighth note pulse. If your students have trouble and are rushing the syncopated rhythms, divide your class in half with some of the students playing the exercise and the others clapping straight eighth notes.

Rhythm Rap teaching sequence: Entire band claps • Add percussion accompaniment • Clap as a round • Sing on "tah".

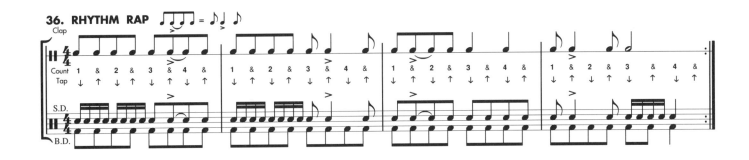

Director · The rhythms of *36. Rhythm Rap* and *37. Syncopation Time* are identical.

NEW NOTES INTRODUCED ON 38. JODIE'S MARCH

Concert B
Concert F# (Oboe)

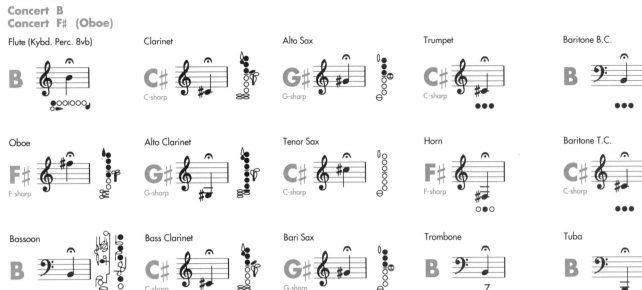

American composer **George M. Cohan** (1878-1942) was also a popular author, producer, director and performer. He helped develop a popular form of American musical theater now known as musical comedy. He is also considered to be one of the most famous composers of American patriotic songs, earning the Congressional Medal of Honor for his works. Many of his songs became morale boosters when the United States entered World War I in 1917.

Director Play the soundtrack or video excerpts from the musical *"George M!"* for your students. This biographical musical pays tribute to the life of this talented man and features many of his favorite songs.

OBJECTIVES FOR 39. ESSENTIAL ELEMENTS QUIZ - YOU'RE A GRAND OLD FLAG

Purpose: Syncopation
Dynamics
Percussion: Rudiment
Identification

Review Exercises: 36. Rhythm Rap
37. Syncopation Time
38. Jodie's March

Percussion: Name the rudiments used in this exercise.

Sixteenth Notes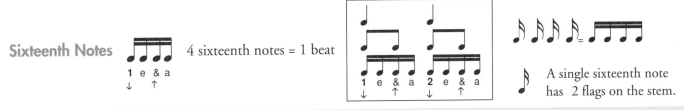

4 sixteenth notes = 1 beat

A single sixteenth note has 2 flags on the stem.

Director The entire band should clap *40. Rhythm Rap.* Percussionists will be able to help teach sixteenth notes since they have already learned them in **Essential Elements** Book 1. Rhythm Rap teaching sequence: Entire band claps • Add percussion accompaniment • Clap as a round • Sing on "tah."

40. RHYTHM RAP

Director The rhythms of *40. Rhythm Rap* and *41. Sixteenth Note Fanfare* are identical. Remind students to be sure to play a full value quarter note on beat four.

41. SIXTEENTH NOTE FANFARE

Director Remind students that good posture and breath support are essential elements for good sound and technique.

Director Students should learn lines A and B separately before playing them together. Encourage listening for good balance of the constant sixteenth note pattern.

43. BACK AND FORTH - Duet

NEW NOTES INTRODUCED ON 44. SHE'LL BE COMIN' 'ROUND THE MOUNTAIN - Variation
Concert C

Oboe

Percussion: Timpani Timpani parts are written in bass clef 𝄢 because the instruments are **tuned** percussion instruments. Each timpani plays one note. To tune each timpani drum, identify the tuning notes from your music. Use an electronic tuner or keyboard percussion instrument, and play one tuning note. Lightly tap your fingers on the head of one drum and compare with the tuning note pitch. Slowly adjust the tuning pedal to match the written note. Repeat for each timpani. Ask your director for assistance. Use medium hard timpani mallets, unless directed otherwise. Timp. is the abbreviation for timpani.

44. SHE'LL BE COMIN' 'ROUND THE MOUNTAIN - Variation

Director   Ask your students to recite the STARS acronym. [Review on Student Book page 3 (Director page 31) if necessary.] Discuss each element of STARS as it pertains to the following exercise.

Percussion: Find all Flamacues and Paradiddles in this exercise.

45. SIGHTREADING CHALLENGE #3   *Review the* STARS *guidelines before sightreading.*

Rallentando *(rall.)* Gradually slow the tempo. (Same as *ritardando*.)

Director Have students learn both lines A and B independently before playing together. Be sure your students learn to watch you closely on the *rallentando*. Remind them to always listen for intonation and balance. Remind your percussionists to try to blend with the band. You should use this warm-up duet often as your students progress through **Essential Elements**.

Percussion: Begin rolls with the right hand and play all ♪'s with the right hand. Next time start with the left hand. Also play this exercise with alternating hands to develop even sounds. Work for smooth rolls.

46. WARM - UP CHORALE - Duet

Director   This is the first exercise in which students move step-wise on the sixteenth notes. Practice at several tempos, teaching your students to play the sixteenths rhythmically even at all tempos.

English composer **Sir Edward Elgar** (1857-1934) received his musical training from his father. Elgar's most famous piece, *Pomp and Circumstance*, was written for the coronation of King Edward VII in 1901, the same year the United States inaugurated its 26th President, Theodore Roosevelt — the youngest man to ever hold the office.

Director Although most students are familiar with the legato theme from this piece often played for graduations and other ceremonies, few will have ever heard the entire *Pomp and Circumstance, March No. 1* by Sir Edward Elgar. Play a recording of this piece for your students and have them identify the two very contrasting sections he uses throughout the piece.

Legato Play in a smooth and connected style, as if all notes were marked with *tenutos*.

48. POMP AND CIRCUMSTANCE - Duet

Sir Edward Elgar

Director Students should be encouraged to practice this exercise on their own striving for the fastest possible tempo, but still maintaining complete *accuracy.* Remind your students to always begin slowly, taking care not to get faster until the exercise is mastered at the slow tempo.

49. TECHNIQUE TRAX

Director   This is the first exercise in which the percussion is asked to play two lines by one player. Although this should be an easy first exercise in independence and fun for your percussionists, you may prefer to use two players initially for the purpose of the quiz.

OBJECTIVES FOR 50. ESSENTIAL ELEMENTS QUIZ

Purpose: **Moving Sixteenth Notes**
Articulation Patterns
Dynamic Contrast
**Percussion: Independence
of Hands**

Review Exercises: **13. Pat-A-Pan**
47. Irish Jig
49. Technique Trax

Percussion: Both snare drum parts should be played by one player.

NEW NOTES INTRODUCED ON 51. CONCERT A♭ SCALE STUDY
Concert D♭
Concert A♭ (Horn)

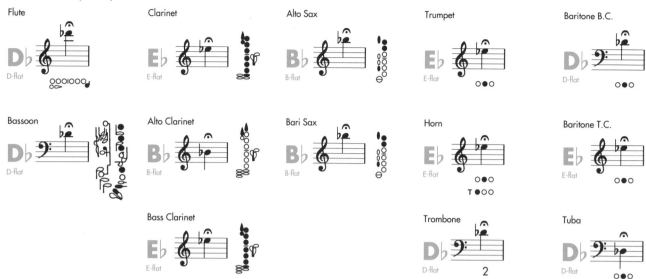

Director Remind students to study the key signature before playing. Your students should begin to memorize both the Concert scale name and the scale name for their own instrument. The individual instrument scale name appears in all student books next to the title of *51. Concert A♭ Scale Study.*

C Instruments: (Your A♭ Scale)
B♭ Instruments: (Your B♭ Scale)
E♭ Instruments: (Your F Scale)
F Instruments: (Your E♭ Scale)
Percussion: (Left-hand wrist builder)

51. CONCERT A♭ SCALE STUDY

Director This *Rhythm Rap* isolates the eighth note followed by two sixteenths. Percussionists learned this rhythm in **Essential Elements** Book 1, and they can help you teach it to the rest of the band.

Rhythm Rap teaching sequence: Entire band claps • Add percussion accompaniment • Clap as a round • Sing on "tah".

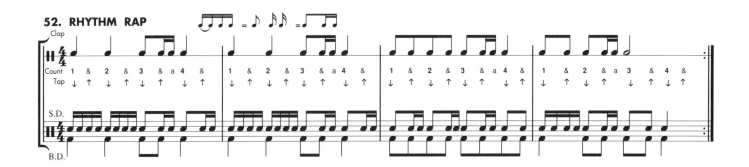

Director The rhythms of *52. Rhythm Rap* and *53. Polka Dot Hop* are identical.

54. SEA CHANTEY

55. AMERICAN PATROL

F. W. Meacham

NEW NOTES INTRODUCED ON 56. CONCERT A♭ REVIEW
Concert A♭

Percussion: Strive for smooth and even rolls.

56. CONCERT A♭ REVIEW

NEW NOTES INTRODUCED ON 57. BILL BAILEY
Concert B♭

Percussion: The suspended cymbal and snare drum should be played by one player using the right hand on the cymbal and the left hand on the snare drum.

57. BILL BAILEY

Hughie Cannon

Director This *Rhythm Rap* isolates two sixteenths followed by an eighth note. Percussionists learned this rhythm in **Essential Elements** Book 1, and they can help you teach it to the rest of the band.

Rhythm Rap teaching sequence: Entire band claps • Add percussion accompaniment • Clap as a round • Sing on "tah".

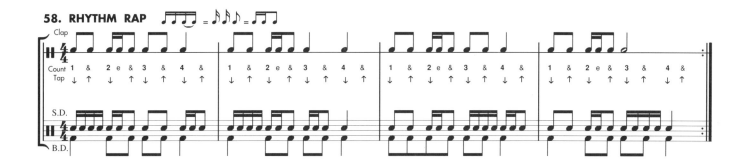

Etude A "study piece" designed to teach a specific musical technique.

Percussion: Both snare drum parts should be played by one player, using the right hand on the rim and the left hand on the head.

Director The rhythms of *58. Rhythm Rap* and *59. Rhythm Etude* are identical.

Percussion: Triangle Roll Roll between the lower closed corner of the triangle using rapid stick motion between the bottom and the side.

60. ENGLISH DANCE

Director You may wish to review *20. Rhythm Rap* before playing this exercise. This is the first time wind and brass players have performed eighth notes in cut time. Be certain to count, clap and tap this exercise with your class before playing.

61. THE THUNDERER

John Philip Sousa

Director Students should carefully study the rhythms in *62. Changing Of The Guard*. This exercise combines both ♫♫ and ♫ as learned in *52. Rhythm Rap* and *58. Rhythm Rap*. You may wish to review these *Rhythm Raps* before playing this exercise.

Percussion: Keep crescendos even. Be careful not to get loud too quickly.

62. CHANGING OF THE GUARD   Count carefully!

Director   Ask your students to recite the **STARS** acronym. Discuss each element of **STARS** as it pertains to the following exercise.

Review the **STARS** guidelines before sightreading.

S — Sharps or flats in the key signature
T — Time signature and tempos
A — Accidentals
R — Rhythm
S — Signs

Percussion: Percussionists should check the music carefully to make sure all instruments and mallets are ready before beginning to play.

63. SIGHTREADING CHALLENGE #4

Director   This *Rhythm Rap* isolates the rhythm of the dotted eighth-sixteenth note.

Rhythm Rap teaching sequence: Entire band claps • Add percussion accompaniment • Clap as a round • Sing on "tah".

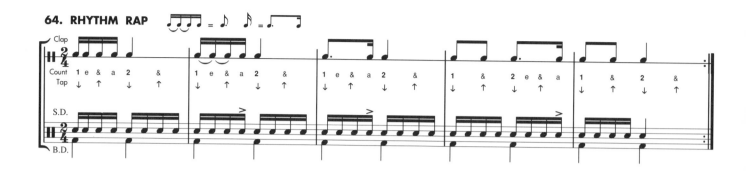

Director   The rhythms of *64. Rhythm Rap* and *65. Marching Along* are identical.

Percussion: Timpani Roll Rapidly alternate single strokes as smoothly as possible. Release on the tied note or final beat.
The hand that starts the roll releases it.

Percussion: Listen to the band's harmony.

67. ARIA FROM THE MARRIAGE OF FIGARO

Wolfgang Amadeus Mozart

French composer **Georges Bizet** (1838-1875) entered the Paris Conservatory to study music when he was only ten years old. There he won many awards for voice, piano, organ, and composition. Bizet is best known for his opera *Carmen,* which was first performed in 1875. *Carmen* showed the new interest of the nineteenth century in the common people; it was about Gypsies and soldiers, smugglers and outlaws. At first people were shocked to see such realism on stage, but *Carmen* was soon hailed as the most popular French opera ever written.

Director   Students should be aware that an opera is a musical dramatic work in which actors sing the dialogue. Operas and musicals continue to be an important part of our culture today. Investigate the possibility of taking your students to see a live opera performance. If you have a college or university near your area, you might be able to find musical theater students willing to come to your school to demonstrate short scenes from operas. Several videos of operas are also available.

OBJECTIVES FOR 68. ESSENTIAL ELEMENTS QUIZ - TOREADOR MARCH FROM CARMEN

Purpose: Dotted Eighth-Sixteenth Rhythm
Demonstration of Maestoso
Famous Opera Music

Review Exercises: 64. Rhythm Rap
65. Marching Along
66. Fanfare For Band
67. Aria from the
Marriage of Figaro

NEW NOTES INTRODUCED ON 69. TANGO - (LA CUMPARSITA)
Concert Gb/F#

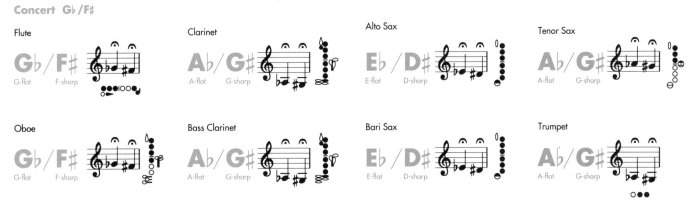

Director   Count, clap, and tap before playing. Stress accurate counting of the syncopated rhythms and the dotted eighth-sixteenth.

Percussion: Listen to how the character of this piece changes in the second half when the rudiments are added.

70. THE YELLOW ROSE OF TEXAS

NEW NOTES INTRODUCED ON 71. CONCERT Eb SCALE AND ARPEGGIO
Concert Eb

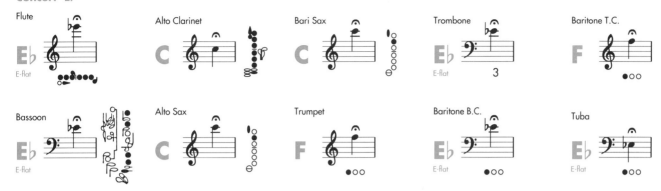

Director   Remind students to study the key signature before playing. Your students should begin to memorize both the Concert scale name and the scale name for their own instrument. The individual instrument scale name appears in all student books next to the title of *71. Concert Eb Scale and Arpeggio.*

      C Instruments: (Your Eb Scale)
      Bb Instruments: (Your F Scale)
      Eb Instruments: (Your C Scale)
      F Instruments: (Your Bb Scale)
      Percussion: Play as a wrist builder using the indicated sticking.

71. CONCERT Eb SCALE AND ARPEGGIO

Director   Remind students to look ahead and study the key change before playing. Point out that good breath support is essential to maintain a good sound on the upper notes.

Percussion: Use paradiddle sticking throughout.

American composer **John Philip Sousa** (1854-1932) was best known for his brilliant band marches. Although he wrote 136 marches, *The Stars and Stripes Forever* became one of his most famous and was declared the official march of the United States of America in 1987.

Director   John Philip Sousa was the most influential person in the development of the march form. Play a recording of any Sousa march performed by a concert band. Discuss the various elements of march form and have your students identify the sections as they hear them.

After performing *73. The Stars And Stripes Forever,* students can participate in the Expert Level of **Music Olympics** found in the **Teacher Resource Kit.** The Expert Level of **Music Olympics** is a fun and challenging review of all concepts learned up to this point in **Essential Elements** Book 2.

Students will also enjoy playing full band arrangements from the **Expert Level** of the **Essential Elements Band Series.** These concert selections reinforce all material learned up to this point in the method. Each student part includes an "Essential Elements" page of valuable review exercises. Call your favorite band music dealer for more information.

NEW NOTES INTRODUCED ON 73. THE STARS AND STRIPES FOREVER
Concert E

73. THE STARS AND STRIPES FOREVER

John Philip Sousa

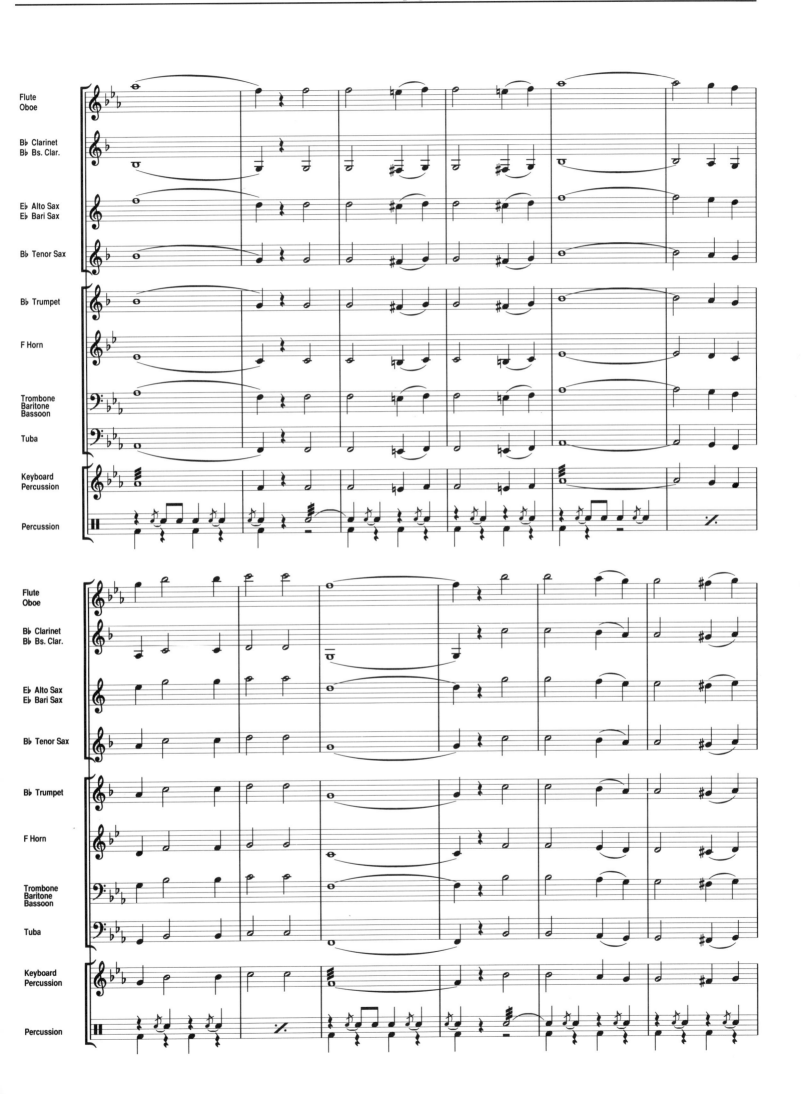

Time Signature
(Meter)

6 - 6 beats per measure
8 - ♪ or 𝄾 gets one beat

♪	= 1 beat
♩	= 2 beats
♩.	= 3 beats
♩⅃	= 6 beats

There are two ways to count **6/8** time:

6 beats to a measure with the eighth note receiving 1 beat.　　OR　　2 beats to a measure with 3 eighth notes (or its equivalent) receiving one beat.

Slower music is usually counted in 6, while faster music is counted in 2. Start by counting 6 beats to a measure, placing a slight accent on beats 1 and 4 when tapping and counting aloud.

Director　This *Rhythm Rap* isolates counting in **6/8** meter.
　　Rhythm Rap teaching sequence: Entire band claps • Add percussion accompaniment • Clap as a round • Sing on "tah".

74. RHYTHM RAP

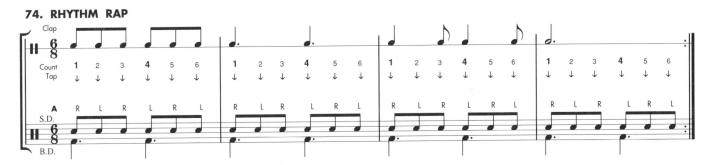

Director　The rhythms of *74. Rhythm Rap* and *75. Lazy Day* are identical. Be sure to count, clap and tap all exercises before playing them.

Percussion: Flam Accent　A snare drum rudiment.

Flam Tap in 6/8 Time　A snare drum rudiment you already know shown a new way.

75. LAZY DAY

76. FRENCH FOLK TUNE

Percussion: Multiple Bounce In $\frac{6}{8}$ Time ♪♪♪ Use the sticking pattern from the eighth note pulse and connect with multiple bounces to sound as smooth as possible.

77. ROW YOUR BOAT The first time through, count and play slowly in 6. Then try playing faster, tapping 2 beats per measure.

78. JOLLY GOOD FELLOW

OBJECTIVES FOR 79. ESSENTIAL ELEMENTS QUIZ - WHEN JOHNNY COMES MARCHING HOME

Purpose: $\frac{6}{8}$ **Meter**
Pick-up note

Review Exercises: **74. Rhythm Rap**
76. French Folk Song
77. Row Your Boat
78. Jolly Good Fellow

79. ESSENTIAL ELEMENTS QUIZ - WHEN JOHNNY COMES MARCHING HOME

Enharmonics Notes that have different letter names but are fingered the same and sound the same. Here is a reference chart for some common enharmonic notes that you will need to know to play the next few chromatic exercises.

Percussion and Keyboard Percussion: Notes that have different letter names but share the same bar on the keyboard percussion instruments. Here is a reference chart for some common enharmonic notes that you will need to know to play the next few chromatic exercises. When playing keyboard percussion, it is very helpful to be familiar with enharmonic notes.

Director Although most of these enharmonics have already been presented, they are listed again here as a review to be used as a reference to help your students play the next few chromatic exercises.

Flute

Oboe

Bassoon

Clarinet

Alto Clarinet

Bass Clarinet

Alto Saxophone

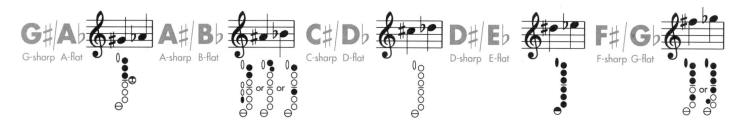

Tenor Saxophone

Baritone Saxophone

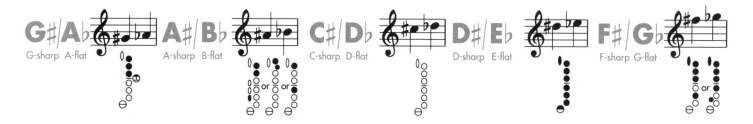

Trumpet

Horn

Trombone

Baritone T.C.

Baritone B.C.

Tuba

Keyboard Percussion

Theory **Chromatic Scale** A scale made up of consecutive half-steps. (A half-step is the smallest distance between 2 notes.) Usually chromatic scales are written with sharps (♯) going up and flats (♭) going down. Practice your chromatic scale to help learn enharmonic notes.

Percussion: The following exercise shows a chromatic scale which you may play on any keyboard percussion.

Director The percussion book includes the keyboard percussion part as well as a snare drum/bass drum part.

Percussion: Play as a snare drum wrist builder using the indicated sticking.

80. CHROMATIC SCALE WARM - UP *Practice slowly at first, until you are sure of all fingerings.*

Director   Students should be encouraged to practice this exercise on their own striving for the fastest possible tempo, but still maintaining complete *accuracy*. Remind your students to always begin slowly, taking care not to get faster until the exercise is mastered at the slow tempo.

Percussion: The top two lines should be played by one player to develop independence of hands.

NEW NOTES INTRODUCED ON 82. HABAÑERA

Concert B

Clarinet

Alternate
fingering

Bass Clarinet

Alternate
fingering

A **Habañera** is a dance in slow $\frac{2}{4}$ meter. It is named after the capital of Cuba, although it was made most popular in Spain during the 1800's by flamenco dancers. One of the most famous Habañeras is heard in Bizet's *Carmen*, written in 1875.

Director   Play a recording of the Habañera from Bizet's *Carmen* for your students. Review the $\frac{2}{4}$ conducting pattern with your students and ask them to conduct along with the recording.

82. HABAÑERA

Georges Bizet

Director Woodwind players should use alternate fingerings in this chromatic exercise. Teach them that these are the correct fingerings to use whenever they encounter similar chromatic passages in their music.

83. CHROMATIC CRESCENDO

Director   Students need constant reminders to use proper breathing and posture. Before playing each exercise, encourage students to demonstrate correct posture when clapping, counting and tapping. A well-supported air stream helps produce the best possible tone on all instruments.

84. TURKISH MARCH

Ludwig van Beethoven

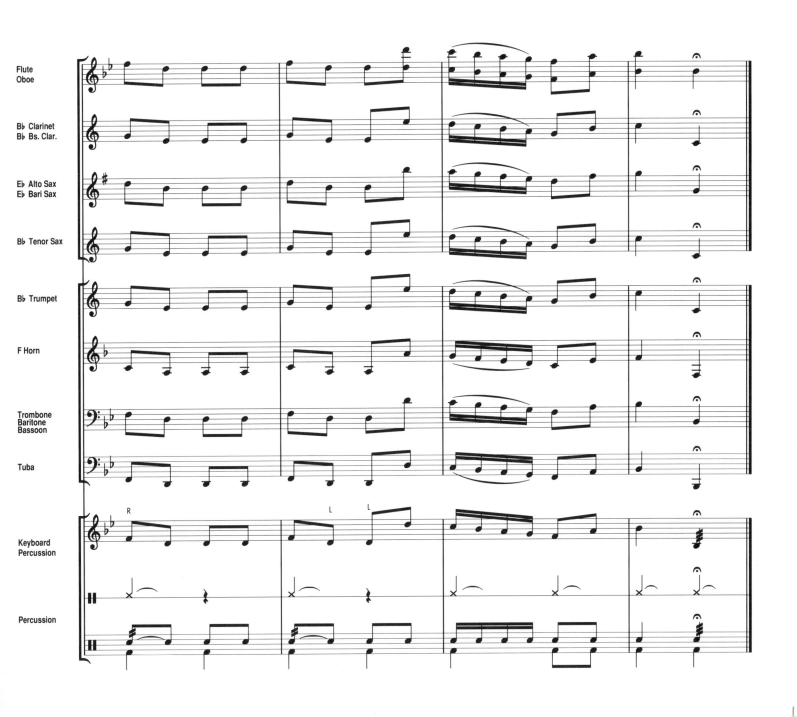

85. THE OVERLANDER

Australian Folk Song

86. STACCATO TIME

Director You may wish to review the history of George M. Cohan found on Student Book page 8 (Director page 72).

87. YANKEE DOODLE DANDY

George M. Cohan

Review the **STARS** guidelines before sightreading.

S — Sharps or flats in the key signature
T — Time signature and tempos
A — Accidentals
R — Rhythm
S — Signs

Percussion: Percussionists should check the music carefully to make sure all instruments and mallets are ready before beginning to play.

Director   Review the **STARS** guidelines with your students, and encourage memorization of this acronym. Discuss each element of **STARS** as it pertains to the following exercise.

Triplets   A triplet is a group of three notes. In $\frac{2}{4}$, $\frac{3}{4}$, or $\frac{4}{4}$ time, an eighth note triplet is played in one beat.

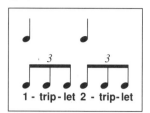

Director   This *Rhythm Rap* isolates eighth note triplets.

Rhythm Rap teaching sequence: Entire band claps • Add percussion accompaniment • Clap as a round • Sing on "tah".

89. RHYTHM RAP

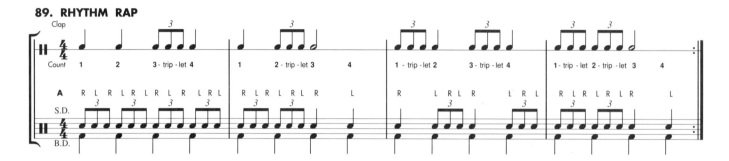

Director   The rhythms of *89. Rhythm Rap* and *90. Three To Get Ready* are identical. Be sure to count, clap and tap all triplet exercises before playing them.

90. THREE TO GET READY

91. CONCERT E♭ SCALE WITH TRIPLETS

Director
Many of your students will be familiar with this famous march from Tchaikovsky's *Nutcracker*. Measures 5 and 6 are purposely written in unison to help students master the low Concert B natural. This is a very difficult note for brass players and they should be encouraged to listen closely to play this note in tune.

You should also work with your students to make sure the dotted eighth-sixteenth rhythm is played accurately so as to not sound like triplets. You may wish to go back and review *64. Rhythm Rap* which isolates the dotted eighth-sixteenth.

92. MARCH FROM THE NUTCRACKER - Duet

Peter I. Tchaikovsky

93. THEME FROM FAUST

Charles Gounod

NEW NOTES INTRODUCED ON 94. CONCERT F SCALE

| **Director** | Remind students to study the key signature before playing. The individual instrument scale name appears in all student books next to the title of *94. Concert F Scale*. |

C Instruments: (Your F Scale)
B♭ Instruments: (Your G Scale)
E♭ Instruments: (Your D Scale)
F Instruments: (Your C Scale)
Percussion: Play as a wrist builder using the indicated sticking.

94. CONCERT F SCALE

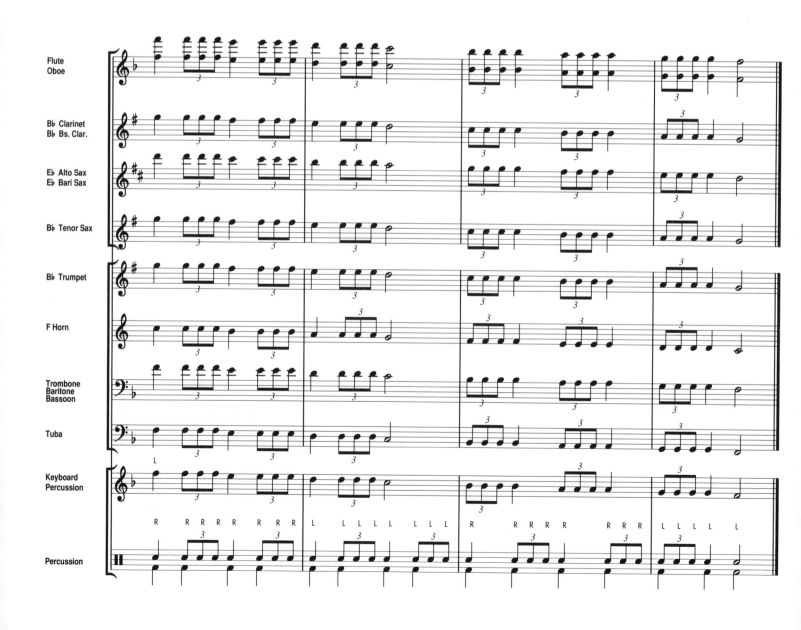

Director Percussionists are encouraged to read two lines simultaneously to develop independence of hands. You should point out to them that they are asked to switch hands in measure 3.

Percussion: The top two lines should be played by one player to develop independence of hands.

95. ETUDE IN THIRDS

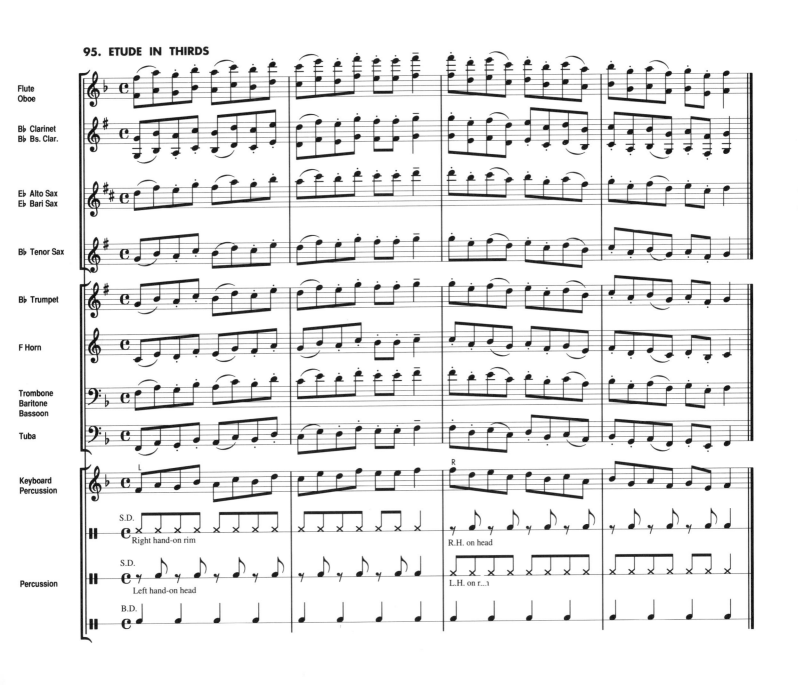

Director This *Rhythm Rap* isolates the rhythm of dotted quarter followed by two sixteenths.

Rhythm Rap teaching sequence: Entire band claps • Add percussion accompaniment • Clap as a round • Sing on "tah".

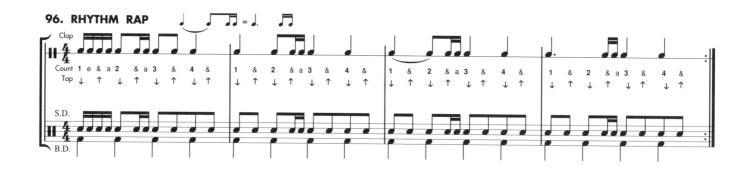

Director The rhythms of *96. Rhythm Rap* and *97. On The Move* are identical.

Director Remind students not to rush the sixteenth notes and to be sure to play all quarter notes with full value. The articulation patterns in each measure are identical. Insist on accurate articulations. Do not allow your students to form the bad habit of ignoring this important element of music.

98. CLIMBING HIGHER

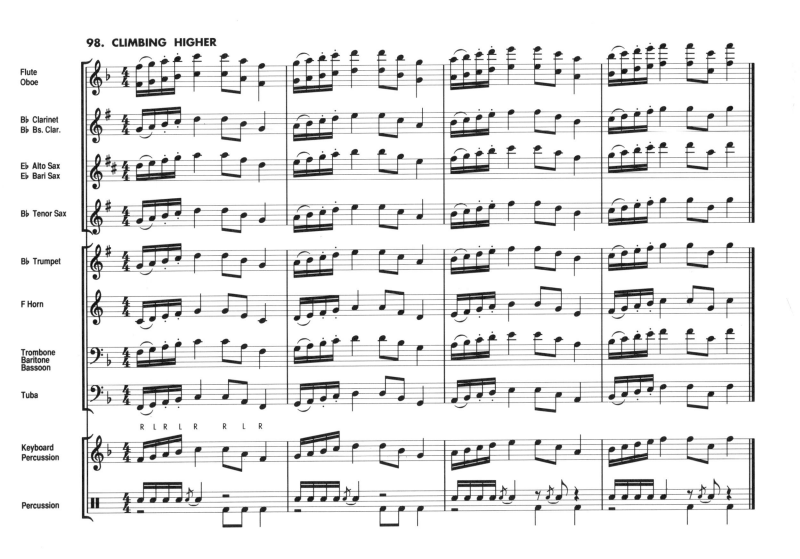

Director
Encourage your students to listen to each other as they play. Stress to them the importance of listening for balance, intonation, and rhythmic ensemble. An effective exercise is to count off *99. Arkansas Traveler* for your students to get started, but then stop conducting. This will force them to listen to each other in order to stay together. Practice this technique with small groups of students as well as with the full band.

Remind your students the importance of working together as a team.

99. ARKANSAS TRAVELER   Remember to tongue lightly.

OBJECTIVES FOR 100. ESSENTIAL ELEMENTS QUIZ

Purpose: Sixteenth Note Rhythm Patterns: **Review Exercises:** 42. Moving Along
                                                                        53. Polka Dot Hop
                                                                        59. Rhythm Etude
                                                                        62. Changing of the Guard
                                                                        97. On the Move

History **The Marines' Hymn** was written in 1847 during the Mexican War by a Marine Corps poet who set the original lyrics to music from an old French opera. Some of the words refer to the Mexican War. The Treaty of Guadalupe Hidalgo (1848) ended the war. By its terms, Mexico recognized the U.S.'s annexation of Texas and California.

Director For centuries bands have played an important roll in patriotism of the United States of America, providing rousing renditions of our nation's Armed Forces songs both in times of peace and war. Besides *The Marines' Hymn*, other Armed Forces songs include: *The Caisson Song* (Army), *The U.S. Air Force Song*, *Anchors Aweigh* (Navy), and *Semper Paratus* (Coast Guard). Many arrangements and medleys of these songs are available for bands. You may wish to add an Armed Forces medley to one of your concerts. It's guaranteed to be a pleaser for your students and audiences alike.

101. THE MARINES' HYMN

Director Students should be encouraged to practice this exercise on their own striving for the fastest possible tempo, but still maintaining complete *accuracy*. Students who are not tonguing properly will have trouble mastering this exercise at the faster tempos. Encourage all students to use a constant air stream, using the tongue only as a valve to release the air stream.

102. TECHNIQUE TRAX Practice slowly at first, then gradually increase the tempo to *Allegro*.

D.S. al Fine Play until you see the *D.S. al Fine*, then go back to the sign (𝄋) and play until you see the word *Fine* (finish). D.S. is the Latin abbreviation for *Dal segno*, "from the sign."

Director Students should already be familiar with *D.C. al Fine* which was introduced in **Essential Elements** Book 1. Explain the difference between *D.C. al Fine* and *D.S. al Fine*. Remind them to always make sure to find the sign BEFORE they begin playing the exercise.

103. D.S. MARCH

Accelerando *(accel.)* Gradually increase the tempo.

Director Review with your students the importance of watching the conductor and listening to the group whenever a change in tempo, such as an accelerando, is encountered. Explain to them to importance of getting faster AS A GROUP when they see an accelerando in their music.

104. CAN - CAN   Jacques Offenbach

▲ Follow your director's accelerating tempo.

Director After your students master this exercise in 6, try in a moderate two. The rhythm ♩♪ ♩♪ is often seen in marches. At this time you may want to begin rehearsing sections of the full band arrangement of *120. Semper Fidelis* found on page 25 of the student books.

Percussion: Play as a wrist builder using the indicated sticking.

105. **⁶⁄₈ STUDY WITH ARPEGGIO**

The **waltz** is a dance in moderate $\frac{3}{4}$ time which developed about 1800 from the Ländler, an Austrian peasant dance. When the waltz was first introduced to the dance floor, it was very controversial because this was the first time partners danced in an embracing position. Austrian composer **Johann Strauss** (1825-1899) composed over 400 waltzes. These include such famous pieces as *The Blue Danube, Tales From the Vienna Woods* and *Emperor Waltz*.

Director Review the $\frac{3}{4}$ conducting pattern with your students and ask them to conduct as part of the band plays *106. Emperor Waltz* or as you play a recording of any waltz for them. If any students know the dance steps to the waltz, you may wish to have them demonstrate this to the class. Although the waltz dates back to the early 1800's, it is still a popular dance today, often performed at formal occasions.

106. EMPEROR WALTZ

Johann Strauss

Director Practice lines A and B separately, then combine in duet ensembles. Review legato style. Students should listen carefully to match the unison pitches on the first and final notes of this duet. The composer of this duet, Johann Christian Bach, was one of Johann Sebastian Bach's twenty-one children.

Percussion: Listen to the band's harmony.

107. ENGLISH DANCE - Duet

J.C. Bach

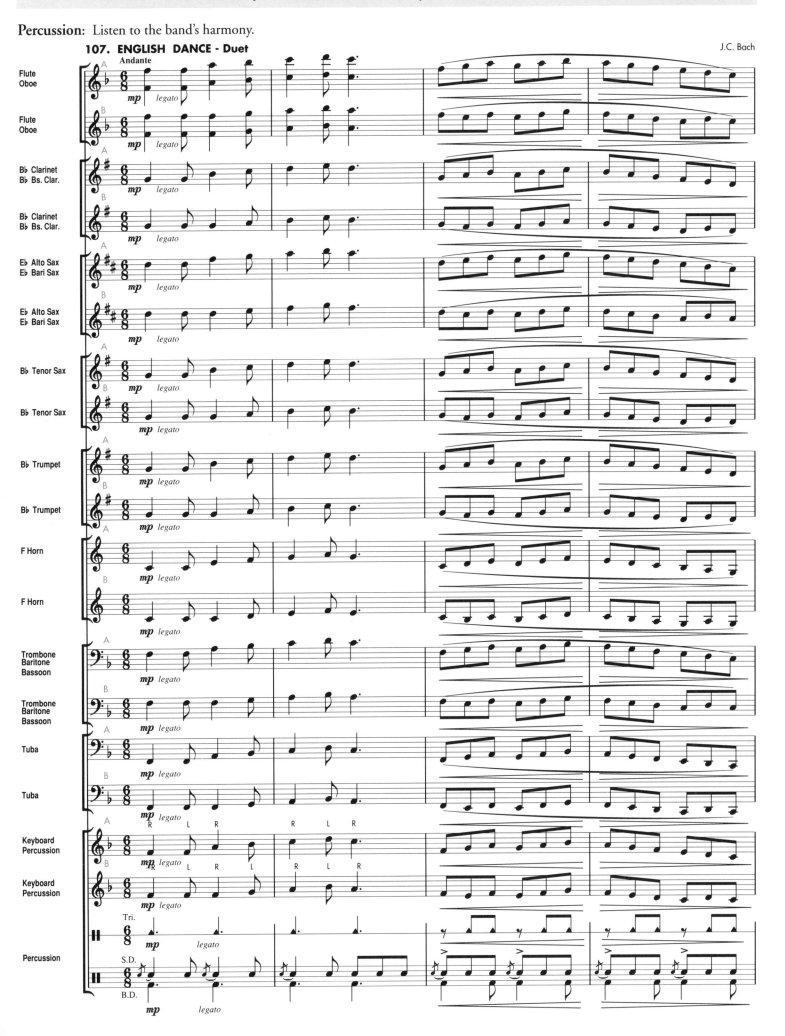

OBJECTIVES FOR 108. ESSENTIAL ELEMENTS QUIZ - BRITISH GRENADIERS

Purpose: Sixteenth Note Rhythmic Patterns:

Dynamic Contrasts
Repeat Signs with
    1st and 2nd Endings

Review Exercises: 47. Irish Jig
                        54. Sea Chantey
                        65. Marching Along
                        97. On the Move
                     100. Essential Elements Quiz

108. ESSENTIAL ELEMENTS QUIZ - BRITISH GRENADIERS

Director Students should be encouraged to practice this exercise on their own striving for the fastest possible tempo, but still maintaining complete *accuracy*. Point out that the articulations in the second half of the exercise are different from the articulations in the first half. Insist that your students play these articulations correctly at all tempos.

Percussion: Play as a wrist builder using the indicated sticking.

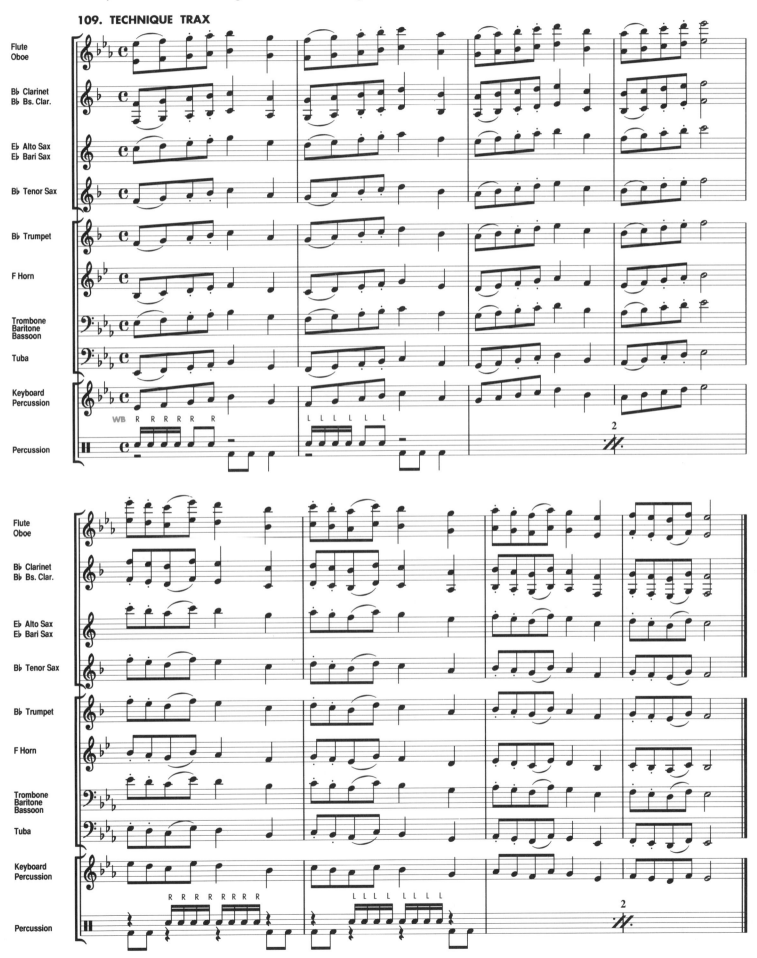

Director Ask your students to define tenuto and then have them demonstrate it by playing *110. Unfinished Symphony Theme.* Special attention should be paid to the last eighth note in measure 7. Remind your students that the accidental at the beginning of the measure carries through the entire measure.

110. UNFINISHED SYMPHONY THEME

Franz Schubert

Director In this very challenging rhythm exercise, the snare drum has the same rhythm as the rest of the band. It will be helpful to have one of your percussionists playing the constant eighth note claves part in order to help the band count together. Make sure your students accurately demonstrate counting, clapping and tapping before they try to play this exercise on their instruments.

111. RHYTHM TRICKS Count and clap before playing.

Measure Repeat Repeat the previous measure.

Director The single measure repeat sign definition does not appear in the Percussion book. This concept was introduced in the **Essential Elements** Book 1 Percussion book.

112. COUNTRY GARDENS

English Folk Song

Director Ask students to identify all syncopated rhythms in *113. Joshua.* The eighth note pattern played by the snare drum will help students count and correctly play their syncopated rhythms.

113. JOSHUA

Black American Spiritual

Director This exercise begins with a pick-up of four sixteenth notes on beat 2. Remind students to play the tenuto quarter notes for full value. Young players may clip these notes short after playing staccato eighths.

114. LISTEN TO THE MOCKINGBIRD Be sure to tongue lightly.

Alice Hawthorne

NEW NOTES INTRODUCED ON 115. RUSSIAN SAILORS' DANCE
Concert C#

Tenor Sax

D-sharp

 Russian composer **Reinhold Gliére** (1875-1956) based his melodies on folk music of the Russian people. Having music reflect the culture of the composer's country was a trend which appeared in much art and music during the late 19th and early 20th centuries. *Russian Sailors' Dance* is an example of such musical Nationalism. It is from his ballet *The Red Poppy,* written in 1927.

Director As a result of revolutions and struggles for independence, the late 19th and early 20th centuries saw the rise of a group of composers whose music expressed the spirit and folk song culture of their homeland. Among these composers were Chopin in his Mazurkas and Polonaises, Listz in his *Hungarian Dances,* Dvorak in his *Slavonic Dances,* and Grieg in his *Norwegian Dances.* Play several of these pieces for your students to help them understand the deep emotion and love for their homeland that these composers were trying to convey.

115. RUSSIAN SAILORS' DANCE

Reinhold Gliére

Go back to the
▼ beginning.

D.C. al Fine

Director Review the basics of cut time. The rhythm of the first two measures of the second ending will present a new counting challenge for your students. Pay special attention to these two measures when counting, clapping and tapping.

116. ANCHORS AWEIGH

Capt. Alfred H. Miles
and Charles A. Zimmerman

Director The numerous accidentals and articulations make *117. Funeral March Of A Marionette* a challenging exercise for all players. After counting and clapping, perform this exercise in six. Gradually work up to a moderate two tempo. Be certain students maintain accuracy and a light performance style.

After performing *117. Funeral March Of A Marionette*, students can participate in the Master Level of **Music Olympics** found in the **Teacher Resource Kit**. The Master Level of **Music Olympics** is a fun and challenging review of all notes, rhythms and terms learned in **Essential Elements** Book 2.

Students will also enjoy playing full band arrangements from the **Master Level** of the **Essential Elements Band Series**. These concert selections reinforce all material learned in Book 1 and Book 2. Each student part includes an "Essential Elements" page of valuable review exercises. Call your favorite band music dealer for more information.

Woodwinds, Brass and Keyboard Percussion: Check all accidentals before playing this piece.

117. FUNERAL MARCH OF A MARIONETTE

Charles Gounod

Director

The following five exercises are FULL BAND ARRANGEMENTS which can be rehearsed at any time throughout **Essential Elements** Book 2. (Please see Special Director Page 12 for a note about these arrangements.) Listed above each arrangement are the new **Essential Elements** Book 2 concepts that are used, followed by the exercise number in which these concepts were first introduced. Refer to these exercises when rehearsing these arrangements to help review and reinforce these concepts with your students. We advise that you pace these arrangements throughout your lessons so that your students have mastered the majority of the corresponding exercises BEFORE attempting the concepts in the full band arrangements. Please note that there are a few new musical terms used in these arrangements that were not introduced in other exercises. These are listed and should be taught by you before rehearsing the arrangement as the definitions do not appear in the student books.

Complete Rehearsal Guides for all **Essential Elements** full band arrangements (Books 1 and 2) are found in the **Teacher Resource Kit.** Each Rehearsal Guide includes simple Rhythm Dictation exercises.

D.S. al Coda Play until you see *D.S. al Coda*, then go back to the sign (𝄋) and play until you see the words "*To Coda*." Skip to the *coda* and play until the end. D.S. is the Latin abbreviation for *dal segno*, "from the sign." *Coda* means "tail" or conclusion.

Director Read the above definition with your class, and be certain students identify the sign (𝄋), *To Coda* and *Coda* markings before playing this piece.

This overture-style arrangement reinforces several musical concepts learned throughout Book 2. These include staccato (ex. 12), *mezzo piano* (ex. 29), syncopation (ex. 36), *rallentando* (ex. 46) and **Maestoso** (ex. 66).

The dynamic *fortissimo* (*ff*) is used in measure 20. Instruct your students that this dynamic means "play very loudly". Band members should play with good sound quality and proper breath support at all dynamic levels.

118. SIMPLE GIFTS - Full Band Arrangement

Shaker Folk Song
Arr. by John Higgins

Director This arrangement allows for expressive, legato playing. New concepts include **Adagio** (ex. 10), tenuto (ex. 14), *ritardando* (ex.15), *mezzo piano* (ex. 29), simple triplets (ex. 89), *rallantando* (ex. 46), and eighth followed by two sixteenths (ex. 52).

Measure 18 is labled "**A Tempo**". Explain to your students that this indicates to play the passage back in the original tempo. This comes after the *ritardando* in measures 16 and 17.

The dynamic of *fortissimo* (*ff*) is used in measure 26. Your students will need to be instructed that this dynamic means "very loud". Be sure you remind you students to play loudly with good breath support and tone quality. Be sure they do not overblow.

119. DANNY BOY - **Full Band Arrangement**

Arr. by John Higgins

Director This rousing march will challenge your students' understanding of $\frac{6}{8}$ meter. We recommend that your students have full mastery of exercises 74 - 79 and especially ex. 105 which teaches the rhythm of ♩.

Percussion has several rolls in this arrangement. Please refer them to the special $\frac{6}{8}$ roll exercises on page 28-B in their student books. Other new concepts students need to be familiar with are staccato (ex. 12) and *simile* (abbreviated in this arrangement as *sim.*) (ex.115).

Special attention should be paid to the *"2nd time only"* instructions at measure 13. The only instruments which play the first time are trumpets and snare drum.

The dynamic of *fortissimo (ff)* is used in measure 26.

120. SEMPER FIDELIS - Full Band Arrangement

John Philip Sousa
Arr. by John Higgins

Student Book page 25

Director This arrangement is a short novelty tune enhanced by several special percussion effects. New concepts include staccato (ex. 12) and **Allegretto** (ex. 15).

Woodwinds should use the alternate chromatic fingerings where indicated in their music. The snare drum alternates between playing on the rim and playing on the drum head.

121. TAKE ME OUT TO THE BALLGAME - Full Band Arrangement

Arr. by John Higgins

Director   Serengeti (An African Rhapsody)

This arrangement will create an exciting close to your concert. Your students will enjoy the African flavor of this piece created by the strong rhythms and interesting percussion effects.

This piece consists of several continuous contrasting sections entitled "Daybreak," "Safari," "Celebration" and "Sunset." Point out and discuss all meter changes, tempo changes and key changes with your students. Remind students to watch you closely and encourage them to always look ahead in their music. Be certain all players understand the special directions in each part at measure 49. This section is to be played three times.

Percussionists are required to play several different instruments throughout the piece. Teach them to look ahead in their music, assign players to the various instruments and set up the entire percussion section before starting the piece. The keyboard percussionist is asked to switch between bells and xylophone if both are available.

Other Book 2 concepts include staccato (ex.12), tenuto (ex.14), *ritardando* (ex.15), *mezzo piano* (ex.29), eighth rest followed by eighth note (ex.30), **Maestoso** (ex.66), and *simile* (ex.115).

122. SERENGETI (AN AFRICAN RHAPSODY)

By John Higgins

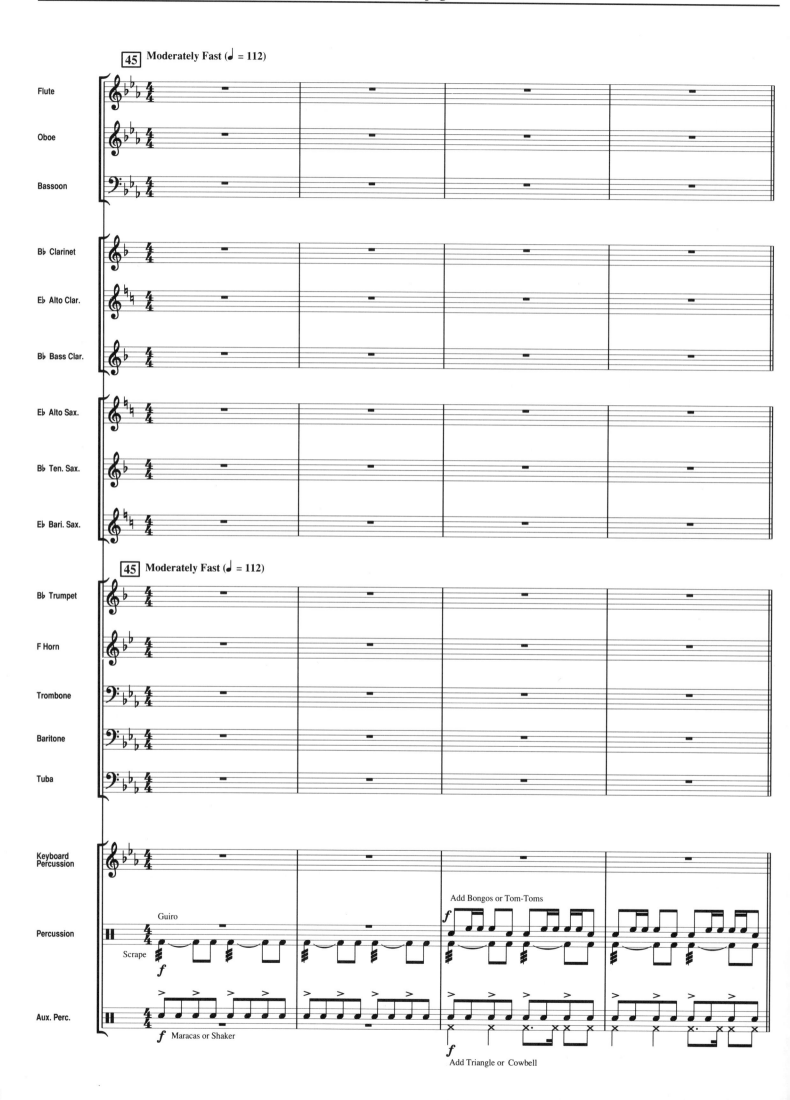

Major Scale   A **Major Scale** is a series of eight notes that follow a definite pattern of whole steps and half steps. Half steps appear only between scale steps 3-4 and 7-8. Every major scale has the same arrangement of whole steps and half steps.

Percussion: The following exercise shows one of the band's most common major scales. Listen as the band plays or play along on any keyboard percussion instrument.

Director The following scale exercises may be used in a full band setting and for individual instrument practice. We recommend that percussionists learn scales on keyboard percussion instruments. In addition, special sticking exercises appear in the percussion book which can be played along with the full band's scales. Percussionists should observe the indicated stickings.

Percussion: Exercises 124-129 allow the band to learn several different major scales. Your director may want you to play major scales also using the keyboard percussion book. Otherwise you may play along on snare drum using the following sticking exercises.

124. CONCERT E♭ MAJOR SCALE (Paradiddles & L.H. Double Paradiddles)

125. CONCERT F MAJOR SCALE (Paradiddles and R.H. Double Paradiddles)

126. CONCERT A♭ MAJOR SCALE (Flamadiddles and L.H. Double Flamadiddles)

127. CONCERT C MAJOR SCALE (Flamadiddles and R.H. Double Flamadiddles)

128. CONCERT Db MAJOR SCALE (Double Sticking)

129. CONCERT G MAJOR SCALE   ("Tricky" Double Sticking)

Director The following chromatic scale may not be used in a full band setting. It is designed for individual study or like instrument groups. It covers the best suitable range for each particular instrument. This scale should be practiced frequently and students should be encouraged to memorize their chromatic scale. The percussion book includes a chromatic scale to be played on keyboard percussion.

130. SPECIAL FLUTE CHROMATIC SCALE

► Refer to the fingering chart in the back of the book if you are unsure of any fingerings.

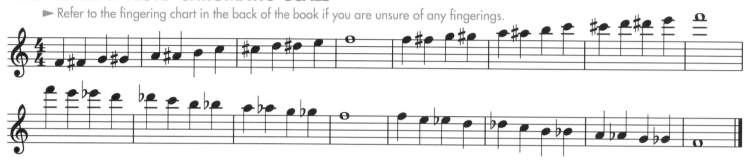

130. SPECIAL OBOE CHROMATIC SCALE

► Refer to the fingering chart in the back of the book if you are unsure of any fingerings.

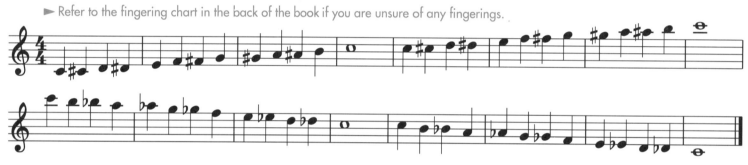

130. SPECIAL BASSOON CHROMATIC SCALE

► Refer to the fingering chart in the back of the book if you are unsure of any fingerings.

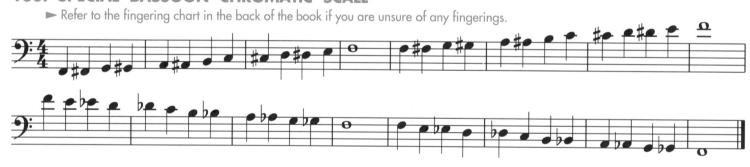

130. SPECIAL CLARINET CHROMATIC SCALE

► Refer to the fingering chart in the back of the book if you are unsure of any fingerings.

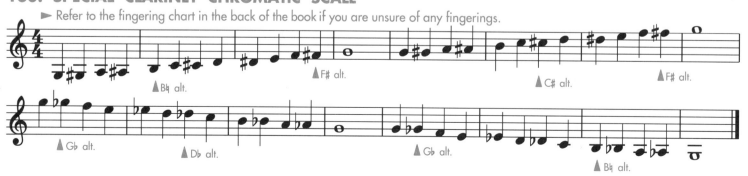

130. SPECIAL ALTO CLARINET CHROMATIC SCALE

▶ Refer to the fingering chart in the back of the book if you are unsure of any fingerings.

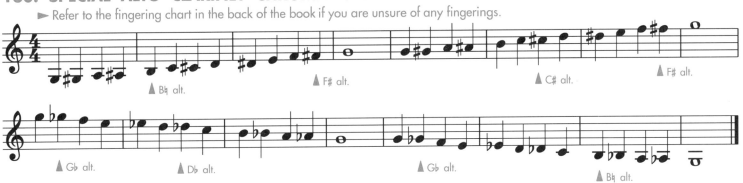

130. SPECIAL BASS CLARINET CHROMATIC SCALE

▶ Refer to the fingering chart in the back of the book if you are unsure of any fingerings.

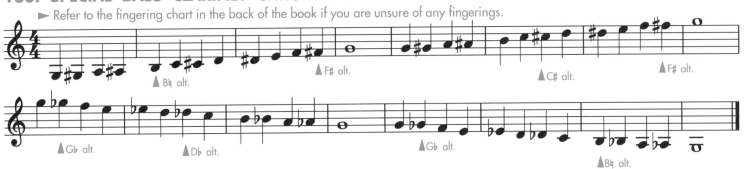

130. SPECIAL ALTO SAXOPHONE CHROMATIC SCALE

▶ Refer to the fingering chart in the back of the book if you are unsure of any fingerings.

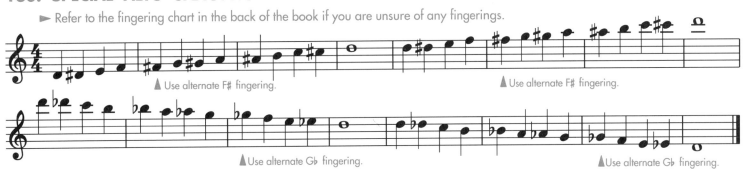

130. SPECIAL TENOR SAXOPHONE CHROMATIC SCALE

▶ Refer to the fingering chart in the back of the book if you are unsure of any fingerings.

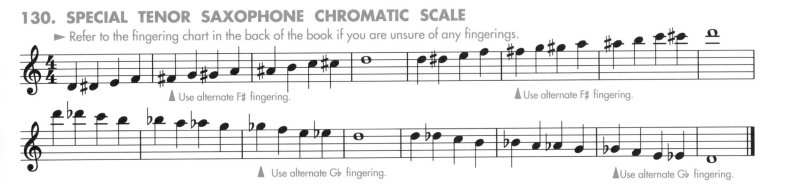

130. SPECIAL BARITONE SAXOPHONE CHROMATIC SCALE

► Refer to the fingering chart in the back of the book if you are unsure of any fingerings.

▲ Use alternate F♯ fingering.　　　　▲ Use alternate F♯ fingering.

▲ Use alternate G♭ fingering.　　　　▲ Use alternate G♭ fingering.

130. SPECIAL TRUMPET CHROMATIC SCALE

► Refer to the fingering chart in the back of the book if you are unsure of any fingerings.

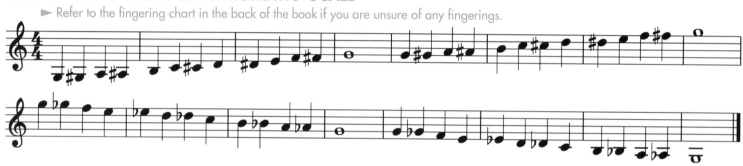

130. SPECIAL HORN CHROMATIC SCALE

► Refer to the fingering chart in the back of the book if you are unsure of any fingerings.

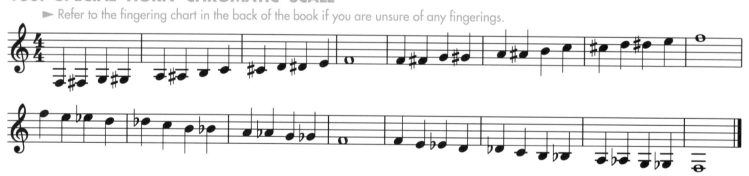

130. SPECIAL TROMBONE CHROMATIC SCALE

► Refer to the position chart in the back of the book if you are unsure of any positions.

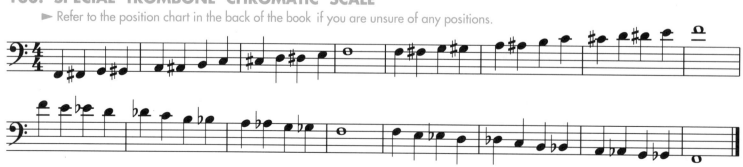

130. SPECIAL BARITONE B.C. CHROMATIC SCALE
► Refer to the fingering chart in the back of the book if you are unsure of any fingerings.

130. SPECIAL BARITONE T.C. CHROMATIC SCALE
► Refer to the fingering chart in the back of the book if you are unsure of any fingerings.

130. SPECIAL TUBA CRHROMATIC SCALE
► Refer to the fingering chart in the back of the book if you are unsure of any fingerings.

130. SPECIAL KEYBOARD PERCUSSION CHROMATIC SCALE
► Refer to the chart on page 29 if you are unsure of any notes.

1st time: R L R L
2nd time: L R L R

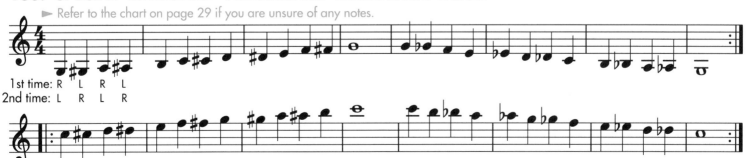

SPECIAL FLUTE EXERCISES

Director   The following Special Exercises are found on Student Book pages 28-29. Teaching suggestions appear on Director page 12 and in **Teacher Resource Kit**.

A. TONE DEVELOPMENT EXERCISE

B. OCTAVE STUDY #1   Keep the octave leaps smooth and connected.

C. OCTAVE STUDY #2

D. ARTICULATION WORK - OUT #1

E. ARTICULATION WORK - OUT #2

F. LEGATO FINGER EXERCISE

B♭

Alternate fingering

G. LOW REGISTER EXCURSION

C

H. RIGHT HAND EXERCISE

C♯/D♭

C-sharp   D-flat

Enharmonic notes. Use the same fingering.

I. INTERVALS

J. ARPEGGIOS

K. ALL NATURAL ETUDE

Andante

mf   *legato*   *f*

▲ Check the key signature.

mf   *f*   *p*

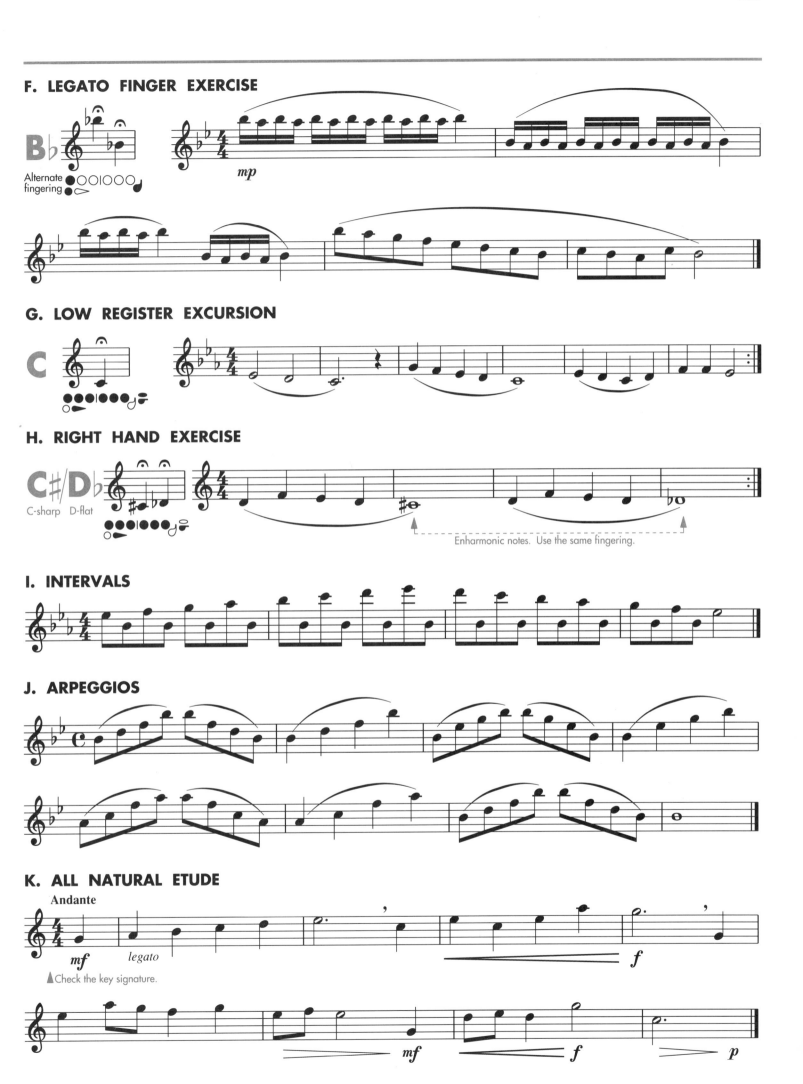

SPECIAL OBOE EXERCISES

A. ALTERNATE EXERCISE #1

R = Right hand Eb
L = Left hand Eb (Alternate fingering)

B. ALTERNATE EXERCISE #2

C. HALF - HOLE EXERCISE

D. ARTICULATION WORK - OUT #1

E. ARTICULATION WORK - OUT #2

F. CHROMATIC EXERCISE #1

G. CHROMATIC EXERCISE IN TRIPLETS

H. STUDY IN CONTRASTS
Moderato

I. ARPEGGIOS

J. BROKEN SCALE   Practice with the following articulation patterns:

A.   B.   C.

K. ALL NATURAL ETUDE
Andante

mf   legato

▲ Check the key signature.

SPECIAL BASSOON EXERCISES

A. LOW NOTE EXCURSION

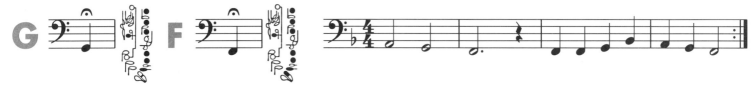

B. ENHARMONIC EXERCISE

C. CHROMATIC STUDY #1

D. ARTICULATION WORK - OUT #1

Allegro

E. CHROMATIC STUDY #2

Andante

F. RANGE REVIEW

G. ARTICULATION WORK - OUT #2

H. LEFT HAND THUMB STUDY Use the proper thumb key.

I. ARPEGGIOS

J. EXERCISE IN 6/8

K. CHROMATIC BASS LINE STUDY

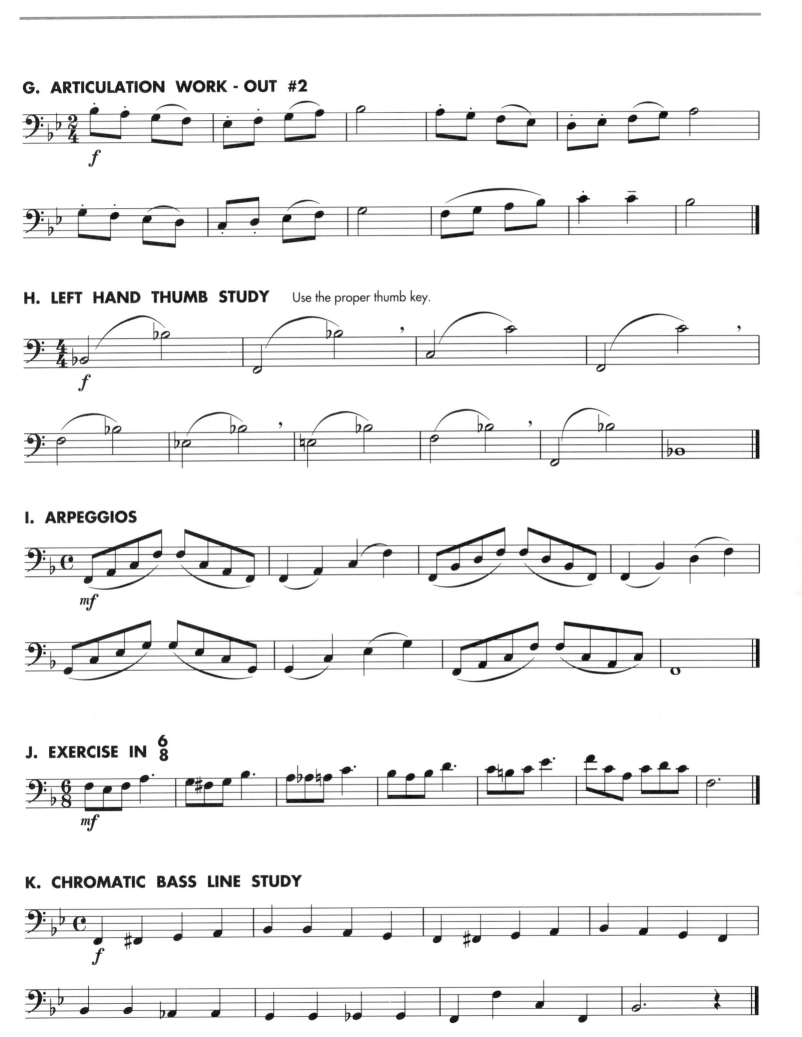

SPECIAL CLARINET EXERCISES

A. CHROMATIC WARM - UP

B. NOTE ADDITION

C. LEFT HAND EXERCISE

Keep right hand down.

R.H. down

D. LITTLE FINGER WORK - OUT   Practice with the following articulation patterns:

► Play all C#'s with right hand little finger.
► Play all B's with left hand little finger.

E. ALTERNATE "C#" REVIEW

F. ALTERNATE "F#" EXERCISE

G. LEFT HAND STUDY

► Use left hand "C" before or after "E♭".

H. ARTICULATION WORK - OUT #1

I. ARTICULATION WORK - OUT #2

J. ALTERNATE "B" REVIEW   Use alternate fingering in chromatic passages.

K. ALTERNATE "F♯" EXERCISE   Use alternate fingering in chromatic passages.

L. RANGE EXTENSION

M. CHROMATIC EXERCISE #1

▲Use alternate F♯ fingering.

N. CHROMATIC EXERCISE #2

SPECIAL ALTO CLARINET EXERCISES

A. CHROMATIC WARM - UP

Slowly

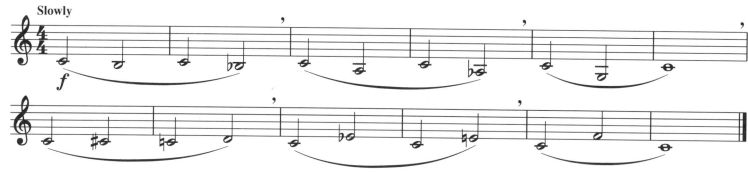

B. NOTE ADDITION

A♭
A-flat

C. LITTLE FINGER WORK - OUT

► Play all F#'s with right hand little finger.
► Play all E's with left hand little finger.

Moderato

D. ALTERNATE "B" REVIEW

Use alternate fingering in chromatic passages.

B
Alternate fingering

E. ALTERNATE "F#" EXERCISE

Use alternate fingering in chromatic passages.

F#
Alternate fingering

F. CHROMATIC EXERCISE #1

G. FLEXIBILITY WORK - OUT

H. ARTICULATION WORK - OUT #1

I. ARTICULATION WORK - OUT #2

J. OCTAVE STUDY

K. LEGATO ETUDE

SPECIAL BASS CLARINET EXERCISES

A. CHROMATIC WARM - UP

Slowly

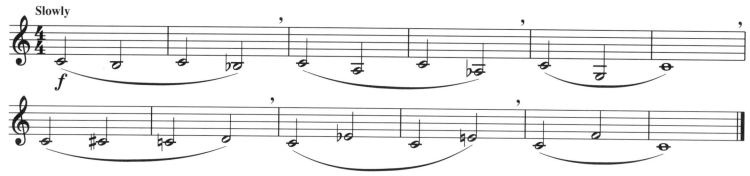

B. NOTE ADDITION

A♭ A-flat

C. LITTLE FINGER WORK - OUT

► Play all F#'s with right hand little finger.
► Play all E's with left hand little finger.

Moderato

D. ALTERNATE "B" REVIEW

Use alternate fingering in chromatic passages

B Alternate fingering

E. ALTERNATE "F#" EXERCISE

Use alternate fingering in chromatic passages.

F# Alternate fingering

F. RANGE EXTENSION

E♭ E-flat

G. ALTERNATE "F" STUDY

Use left hand F when coming from or going to A♭ or E♭.

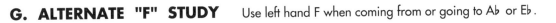

H. ARTICULATION WORK - OUT #1

I. ARTICULATION WORK - OUT #2

J. OCTAVE STUDY

Use alternate F fingering.

K. LEGATO ETUDE

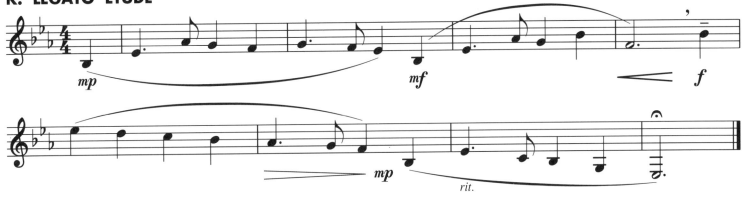

SPECIAL ALTO SAXOPHONE EXERCISES

A. RANGE EXTENSION #1

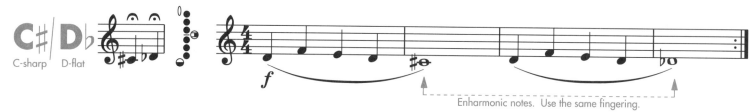

Enharmonic notes. Use the same fingering.

B. RANGE EXTENSION #2

C. LOW REGISTER STUDY

D. ARTICULATION WORK - OUT #1

E. ARTICULATION WORK - OUT #2

F. B♭ EXERCISE #1

Alternate fingering

G. B♭ EXERCISE #2

Alternate fingering

SPECIAL TENOR SAXOPHONE EXERCISES

A. RANGE EXTENSION

Enharmonic notes. Use the same fingering.

B. RANGE REVIEW

C. LOW REGISTER STUDY

D. ARTICULATION WORK - OUT #1

E. ARTICULATION WORK - OUT #2

F. B♭ EXERCISE #1

G. B♭ EXERCISE #2

H. INTERVAL STUDY #1

I. INTERVAL STUDY #2

J. CHROMATIC TRIPLET EXERCISE

K. NOTE ADDITION

L. ARPEGGIOS

M. F# EXERCISE #1   Use the alternate F# where indicated by the ▲.

N. F# EXERCISE #2   Use the alternate F# only where indicated by the ▲.

SPECIAL BARITONE SAXOPHONE EXERCISES

A. RANGE EXTENSION #1

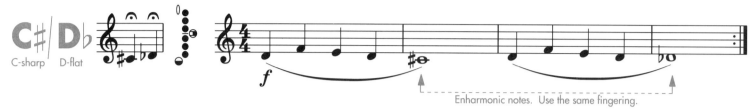

Enharmonic notes. Use the same fingering.

B. RANGE EXTENSION #2

C. LOW REGISTER STUDY

D. ARTICULATION WORK - OUT #1

E. ARTICULATION WORK - OUT #2

F. Bb EXERCISE #1

Alternate fingering

G. Bb EXERCISE #2

Alternate fingering

H. INTERVAL STUDY #1

I. INTERVAL STUDY #2

J. CHROMATIC TRIPLET EXERCISE

K. NOTE ADDITION

A-flat

L. ARPEGGIOS

M. F# EXERCISE #1
Use the alternate F# only where indicated by the ▲

Alternate fingering

N. F# EXERCISE #2
Use the alternate F# only where indicated by the ▲

Alternate fingering

SPECIAL TRUMPET EXERCISES

A. LOW NOTE EXCURSION

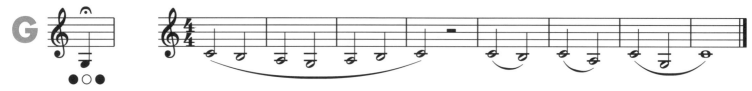

B. ENHARMONIC EXERCISE

G♯/A♭
G-sharp A-flat

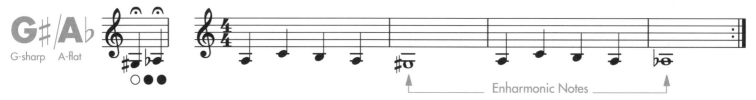

Enharmonic Notes

C. TONE DEVELOPMENT EXERCISE

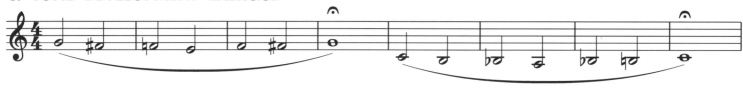

D. ARTICULATION WORK - OUT

E. FLEXIBILITY FUN #1   Use the fingerings which are indicated.

F. FLEXIBILITY FUN #2

G. FINGER TANGLER #1

H. FINGER TANGLER #2

I. FINGER TANGLER #3

▲ Check the key signature.

J. INTERVALS

K. CHROMATICS

L. TONGUE TRAINER   Practice slowly at first, then gradually increase the tempo.

M. RANGE BUILDER

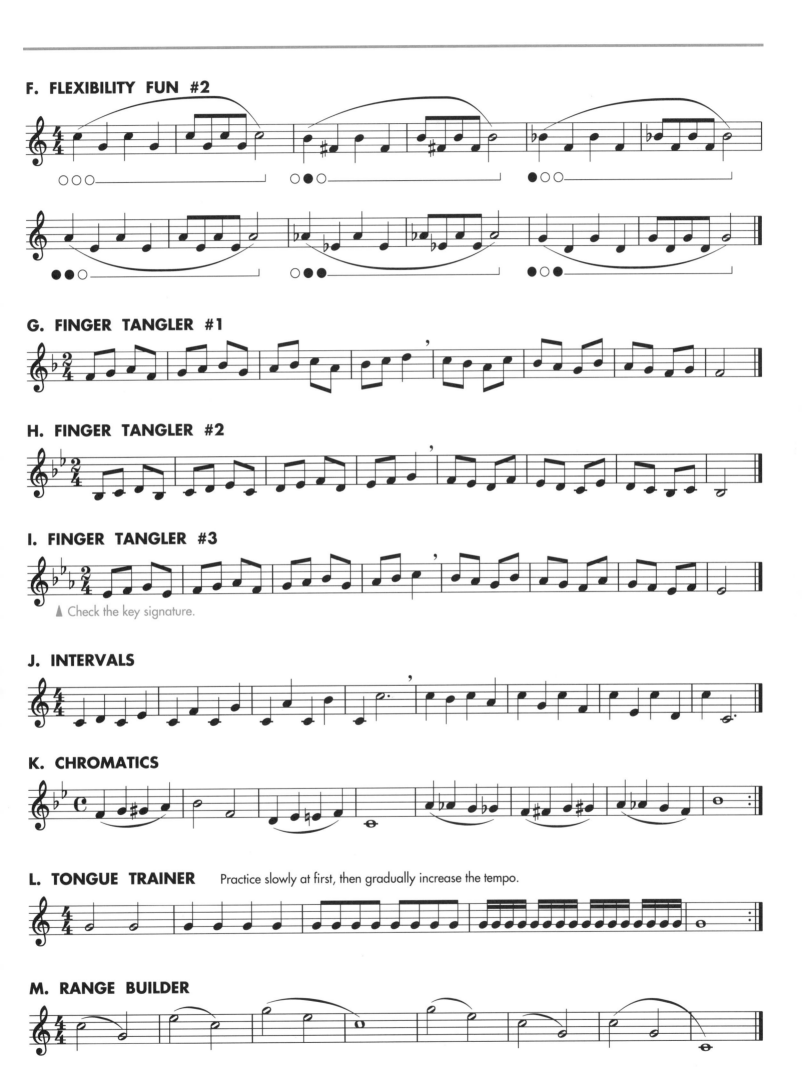

SPECIAL HORN EXERCISES

A. TONE DEVELOPMENT EXERCISE

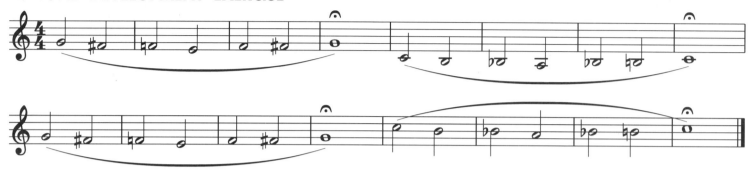

B. LOW NOTE EXCURSION

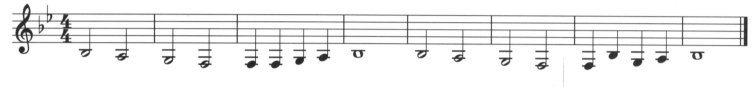

C. ARTICULATION WORK - OUT

D. FLEXIBILITY FUN #1

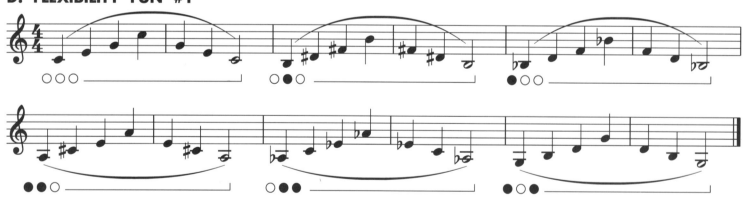

E. LEGATO ETUDE

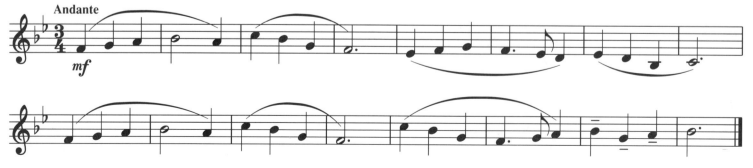

F. TWO NEW NOTES

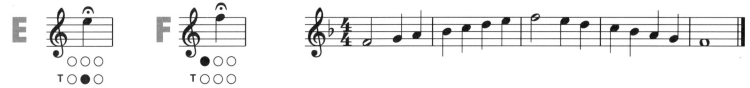

G. FLEXIBILITY FUN #2

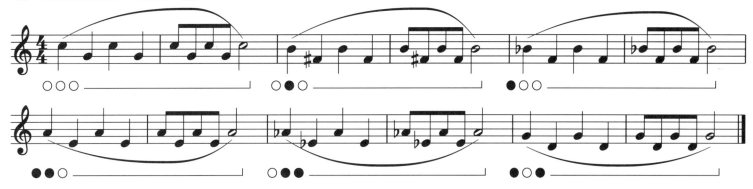

H. CHROMATICS

I. FINGER TANGLER #1

J. FINGER TANGLER #2

K. FINGER TANGLER #3

▲ Check the key signature.

L. INTERVALS

M. TONGUE TRAINER   Practice slowly at first, then gradually increase the tempo.

SPECIAL TROMBONE EXERCISES

A. LOW NOTE EXCURSION

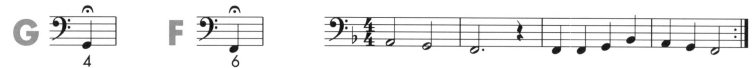

B. ENHARMONIC EXERCISE

C. TONE DEVELOPMENT EXERCISE

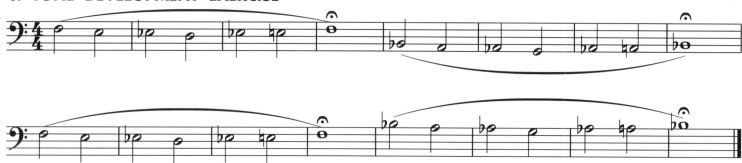

Alternate Positions Many notes on the trombone can be played with different (or alternate) positions. Alternate positions can sometimes help you to play with less slide movement. The most common alternate position is demonstrated below.

D. ALTERNATE F

E. ALTERNATE PRACTICE

F. FLEXIBILITY FUN #1   Use the positions which are indicated.

G. FLEXIBILITY FUN #2

H. CHROMATICS

I. SLIDE WORK - OUT #1   Watch for alternate positions.

J. SLIDE WORK - OUT #2   Move your slide quickly between each note.

K. SLIDE WORK - OUT #3   Play all 2nd positions correctly.

L. TONGUE TRAINER   Practice slowly at first, then gradually increase the tempo.

M. RANGE BUILDER

SPECIAL BARITONE B.C. EXERCISES

A. LOW NOTE EXCURSION

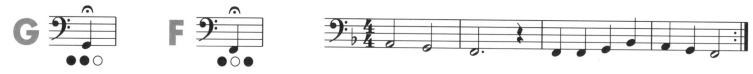

B. ENHARMONIC EXERCISE

F-sharp   G-flat

Enharmonic notes

C. TONE DEVELOPMENT EXERCISE

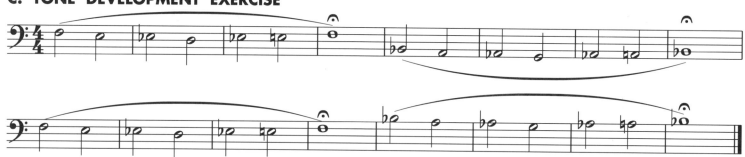

D. ARTICULATION WORK - OUT

mf

E. FLEXIBILITY FUN #1   Use the fingerings which are indicated.

F. FLEXIBILITY FUN #2

G. FINGER TANGLER #1

H. FINGER TANGLER #2

I. FINGER TANGLER #3

▲ Check the key signature.

J. CHROMATICS

K. INTERVALS

L. TONGUE TRAINER   Practice slowly at first, then gradually increase the tempo.

M. RANGE BUILDER

SPECIAL BARITONE T.C. EXERCISES

A. LOW NOTE EXCURSION

B. ENHARMONIC EXERCISE

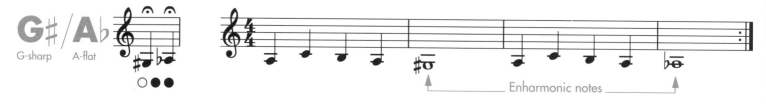

C. TONE DEVELOPMENT EXERCISE

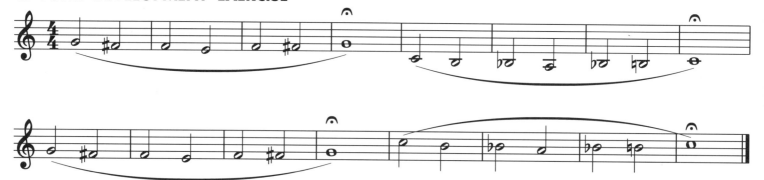

D. ARTICULATION WORK - OUT

E. FLEXIBILITY FUN #1   Use the fingerings which are indicated.

SPECIAL TUBA EXERCISES

A. LOW NOTE EXCURSION

B. ENHARMONIC EXERCISE

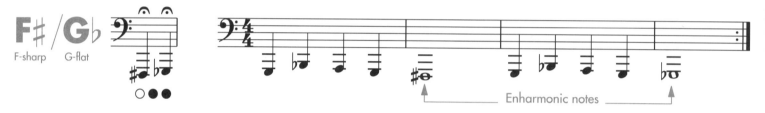

Enharmonic notes

C. INTERVALS

D. ARTICULATION WORK - OUT

E. FLEXIBILITY FUN #1

F. FLEXIBILITY FUN #2

G. TONE DEVELOPMENT EXERCISE

H. CHROMATICS

I. TONGUE TRAINER
Practice slowly at first, then gradually increase the tempo.

J. RANGE BUILDER

K. FINGER TANGLER #1

L. FINGER TANGLER #2

M. FINGER TANGLER #3

▲ Check the key signature.

SPECIAL KEYBOARD PERCUSSION EXERCISES

A. INTERVALS

B. OCTAVES

C. ARPEGGIO ENCOUNTER #1

D. ARPEGGIO ENCOUNTER #2

E. STEP - WISE TRIPLETS

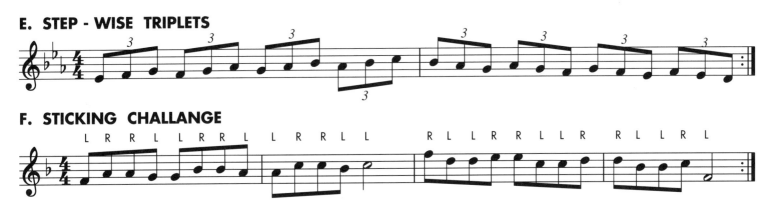

F. STICKING CHALLANGE

Double Stops Playing two notes at the same time. When playing double stops, strive for equal balance between both notes and consistent mallet height.

G. DOUBLE STOPS EXERCISE #1

H. DOUBLE STOPS EXERCISE #2

KEYBOARD PERCUSSION NOTE CHART

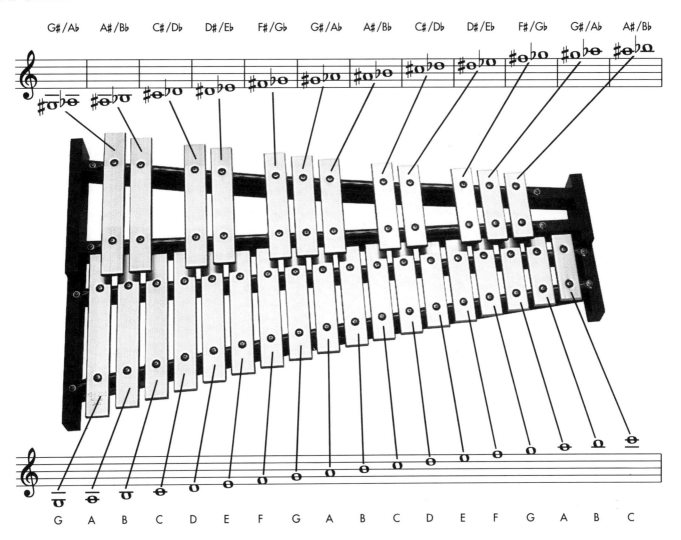

SPECIAL PERCUSSION EXERCISES

ROLL REVIEW EXERCISES

The following roll exercises will help you become more familiar with the basic hand motion required to play smooth sounding rolls. Each roll exercise is divided into two parts. (You will see a thin double bar line dividing the two parts.) Playing the first part of each exercise with the correct hand motion will prepare you for the correct playing of the rolls in the second part of the exercise. Remember: Your hand motion should be the same in both parts of the exercise. The only difference is that you add multiple or double bounces to the sixteenth note hand motion when you play the rolls.

Rolls in Cut Time   When playing rolls in cut time, add multiple or double bounces to the eighth note hand motion.

ADDITIONAL STUDIES IN $\frac{6}{8}$ METER

It is very important for percussionists to be familiar with sixteenth notes in $\frac{6}{8}$ meter since this is the rhythmic pulse for playing rolls in $\frac{6}{8}$. Play the following exercises slowly at first, then gradually increase your tempo. Use alternate sticking patterns unless your director tells you otherwise.

EXERCISES IN PLAYING ACCENTS

Playing accents in the correct places in your music not only makes your part more interesting, but also helps the rest of the band play their parts better. Pay very close attention to the accents while playing the next exercises. Start these exercises slowly at first, then gradually increase your tempo.

A. ACCENT CHALLENGE #1

B. ACCENT CHALLENGE #2

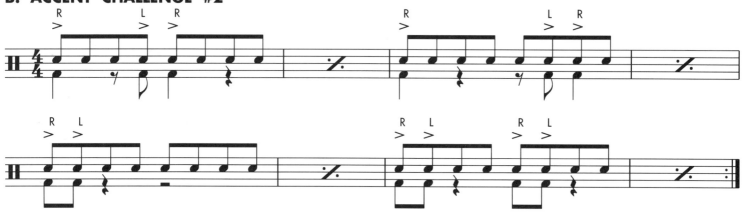

C. ACCENT CHALLENGE #3

EXERCISES IN INDEPENDENCE

The following exercises will help you to develop the ability to play more than one line of music at the same time. This is a very valuable skill for all percussionists to learn. On the next three exercises, the top line of music should be played with your right hand, while the bottom line should be played with your left hand. Use two drums with different pitches or use one drum with one hand playing on the head of the drum and the other hand playing on the rim.

A. INDEPENDENCE WORK - OUT #1

B. INDEPENDENCE WORK - OUT #2

C. INDEPENDENCE WORK - OUT #3

D. INDEPENDENCE WORK - OUT #4

FLUTE FINGERING CHART

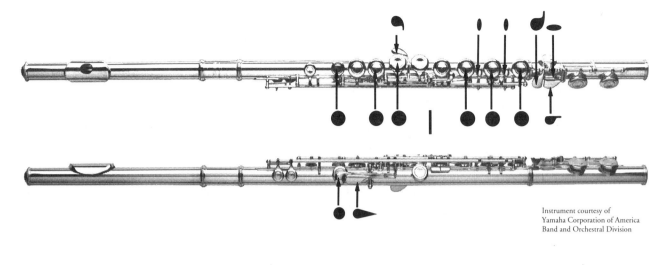

Instrument courtesy of
Yamaha Corporation of America
Band and Orchestral Division

◯ = OPEN

● = PRESSED DOWN

The most common fingering appears on top
when two fingerings are shown.

Take Special Care

Before putting your instrument back in its case after playing, do the following:
- Carefully shake the water out of the head joint.
- Put a clean soft cloth on the end of your cleaning rod.
- Draw the cleaning cloth and rod through the middle and foot joints.
- Carefully wipe the outside of each section to keep the finish clean.

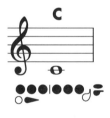

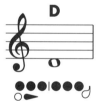

OBOE FINGERING CHART

Take Special Care

Before putting your instrument back in its case after playing, do the following:

- Carefully remove the reed and blow air through it. Return to reed case.
- Take the instrument apart in the reverse order of assembly. Swab out each section with a cloth or feather swab. If the cloth swab has a weight on one end, drop the weight through each section and pull through. Return each section to the correct spot in the case.

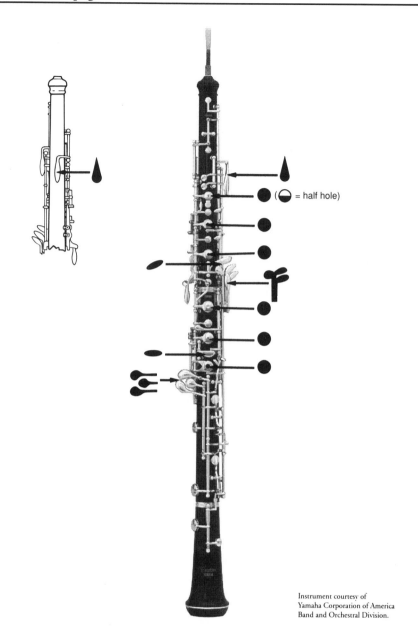

(◐ = half hole)

○ = OPEN

● = PRESSED DOWN

◐ = HALF HOLE COVERED

The most common fingering appears first when two fingerings are shown.

Instrument courtesy of
Yamaha Corporation of America
Band and Orchestral Division.

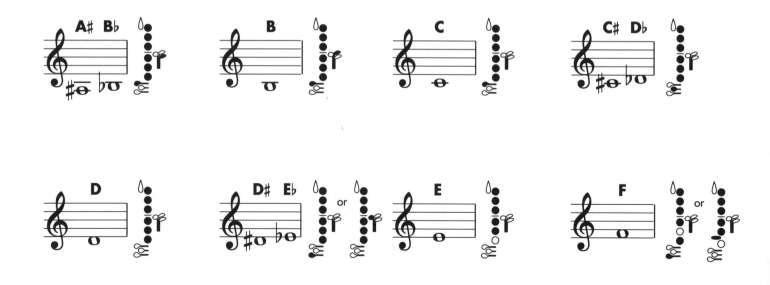

BASSOON FINGERING CHART

Take Special Care

Before putting your instrument back in its case after playing, do the following:

- Carefully remove the reed and blow air through it. Return to reed case.
- Remove the bocal and blow air through one end to remove excess moisture.
- Take the instrument apart in the reverse order of assembly. Swab out each section with a cloth swab or cleaning rod. Drop the weight of the swab through each section and pull it through. Return each section to the correct spot in the case.

= OPEN

= PRESSED DOWN

= HALF HOLE COVERED

The most common fingering appears first when two fingerings are shown.

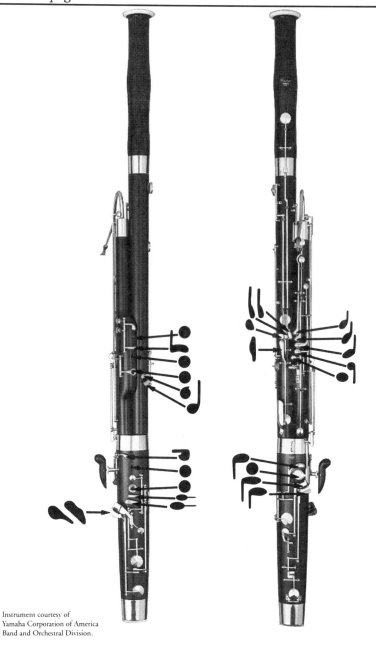

Instrument courtesy of
Yamaha Corporation of America
Band and Orchestral Division.

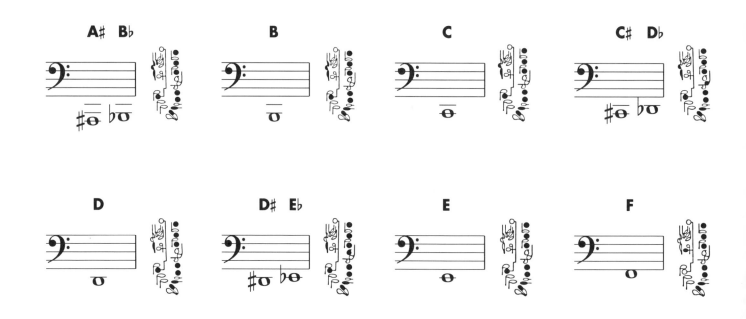

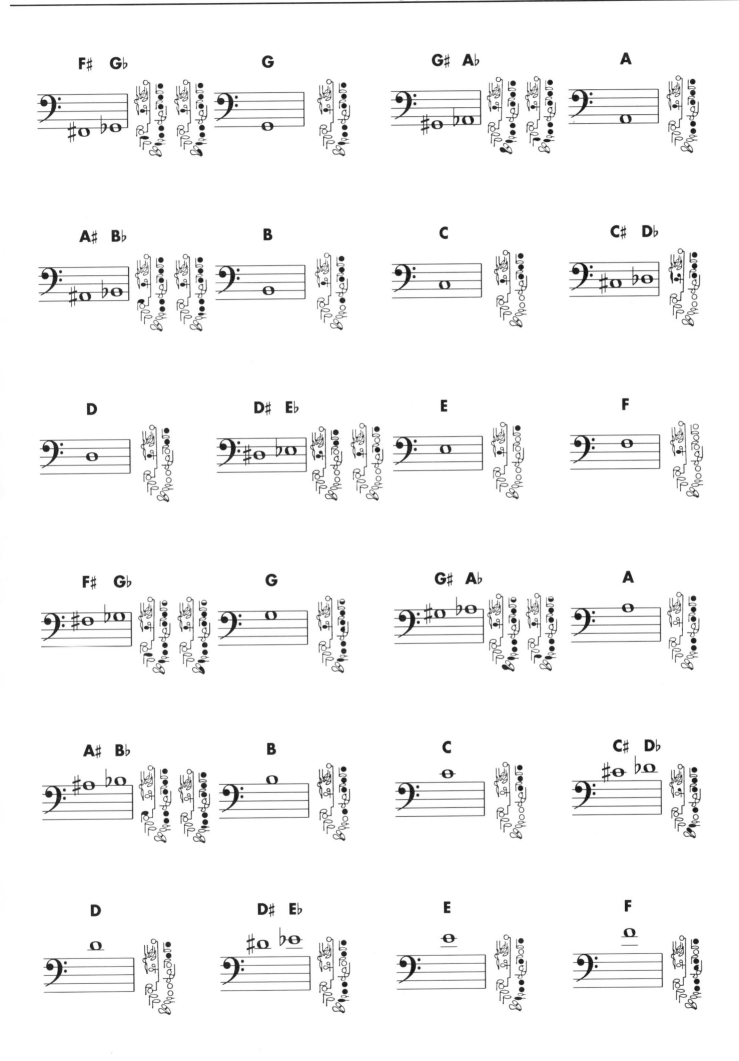

Bb CLARINET FINGERING CHART

Take Special Care

Before putting your instrument back in its case after playing, do the following:

- Remove the reed and wipe off excess moisture. Return to reed case.
- Remove mouthpiece and wipe the inside with a clean cloth. Wash your mouthpiece once per week with warm tap water. Dry thoroughly.
- Hold the upper section with your left hand and the lower section with your right hand. Gently twist the sections apart. Shake out excess moisture.
- Drop the weight of the chamois or cotton swab and pull through each section. Carefully twist barrel and bell from each section, and place in the instrument case.

 = OPEN

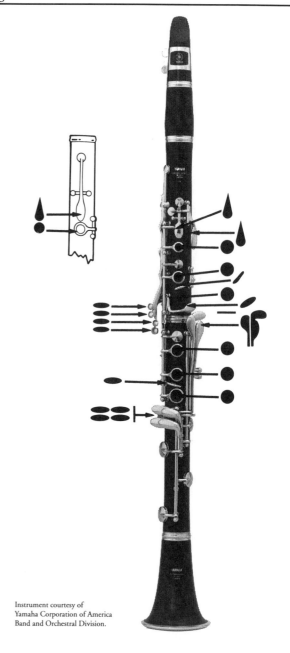

Instrument courtesy of
Yamaha Corporation of America
Band and Orchestral Division.

= PRESSED DOWN

The most common fingering appears first when two fingerings are shown.

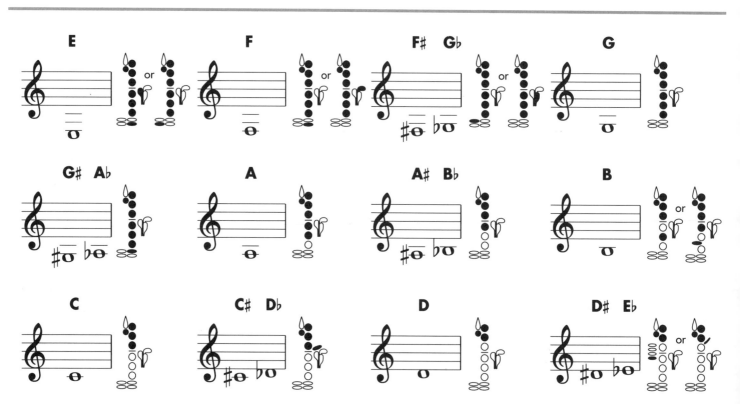

E♭ ALTO CLARINET FINGERING CHART

Take Special Care

Before putting your instrument back in its case after playing, do the following:

- Remove the reed and wipe off excess moisture. Return to reed case.
- Remove mouthpiece and wipe the inside with a clean cloth. Wash your mouthpiece once per week with warm tap water. Dry thoroughly.
- Remove the neck and bell, and shake out excess moisture. Hold the upper section with your left hand and the lower section with your right hand. Gently twist the sections apart. Shake out excess moisture.
- Drop the weight of the chamois cotton swab and pull through each section. Return the instrument to its case.

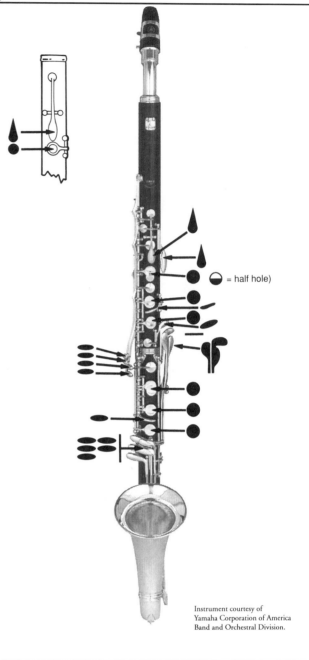

⬤ = half hole)

O = OPEN

⬤ = PRESSED DOWN

The most common fingering appears first when two fingerings are shown.

Instrument courtesy of
Yamaha Corporation of America
Band and Orchestral Division.

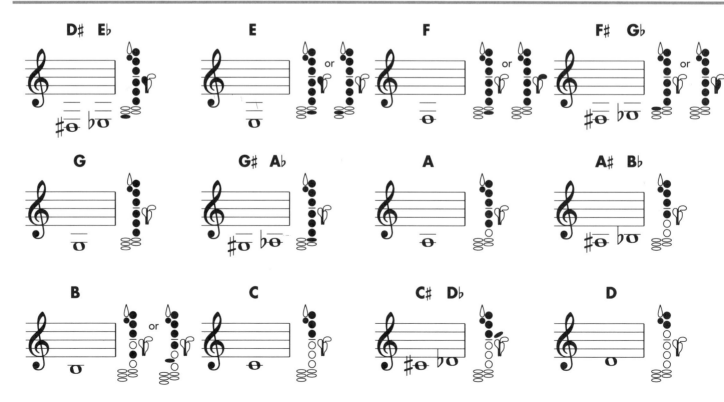

Bb BASS CLARINET FINGERING CHART

Take Special Care

Before putting your instrument back in its case after playing, do the following:

- Remove the reed and wipe off excess moisture. Return to reed case.
- Remove mouthpiece and wipe the inside with a clean cloth. Wash your mouthpiece once per week with warm tap water. Dry thoroughly.
- Remove the neck and bell, and shake out excess moisture. Hold the upper section with your left hand and the lower section with your right hand. Gently twist the sections apart. Shake out excess moisture.
- Drop the weight of the chamois or cotton swab and pull through each section. Return the instrument to its case.

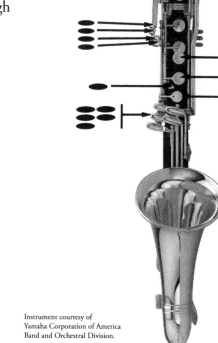

(◖ = half hole)

○ = OPEN

● = PRESSED DOWN

The most common fingering appears first when two fingerings are shown.

Instrument courtesy of
Yamaha Corporation of America
Band and Orchestral Division.

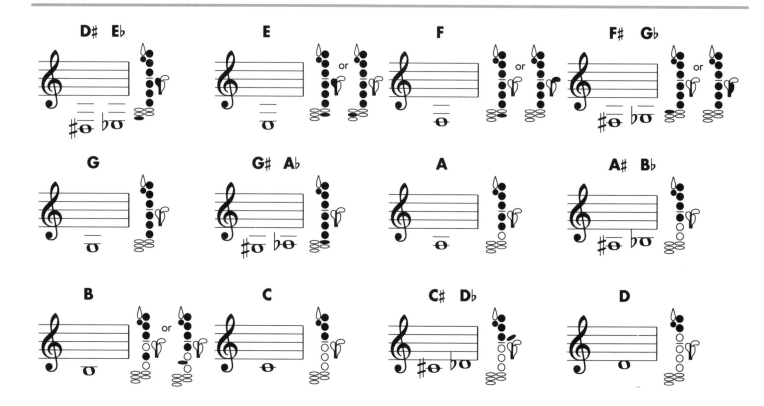

Eb ALTO SAXOPHONE FINGERING CHART

Take Special Care

Before putting your instrument back in its case after playing, do the following:

- Remove the reed and wipe off excess moisture. Return to reed case.
- Remove mouthpiece and wipe the inside with a clean cloth. Wash your mouthpiece once per week with warm tap water. Dry thoroughly.
- Remove the neck and shake out excess moisture. Dry with neck cleaner.
- Drop the weight of the chamois or cotton swab into the bell. Pull the swab through the body several times. Return the instrument to its case.

O = OPEN

● = PRESSED DOWN

The most common fingering appears first when two fingerings are shown.

Instrument courtesy of
Yamaha Corporation of America
Band and Orchestral Division.

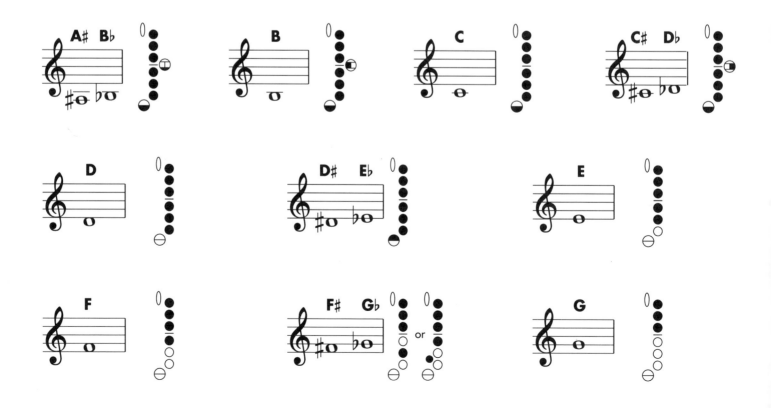

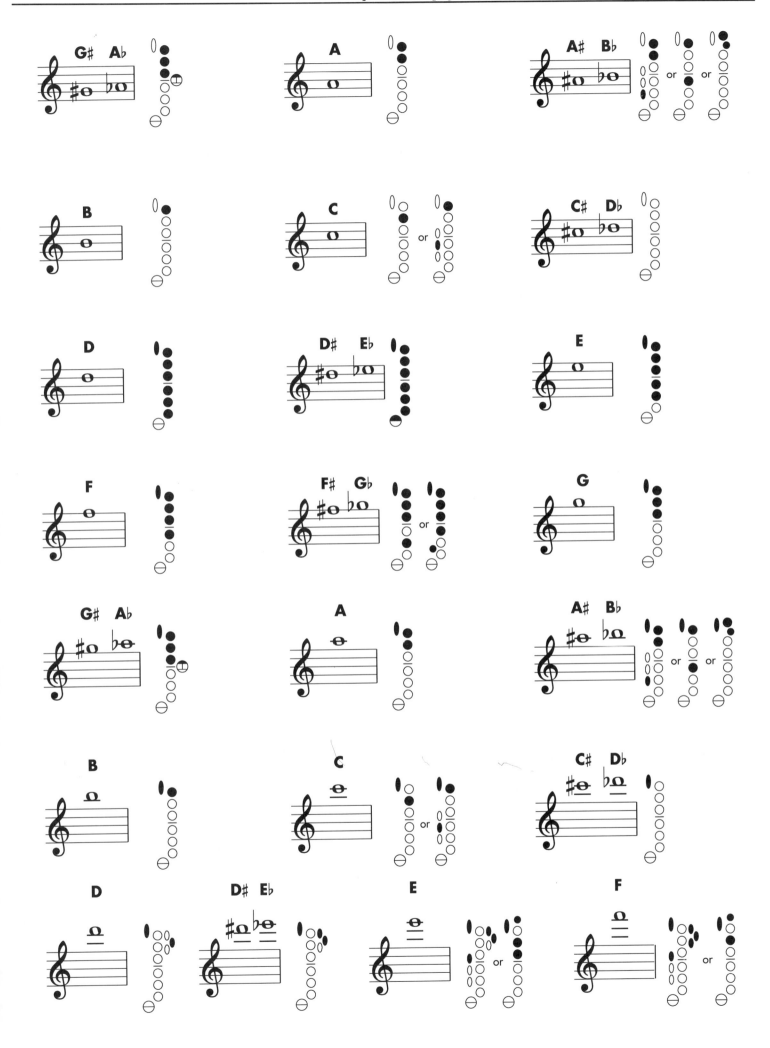

B♭ TENOR SAXOPHONE FINGERING CHART

Take Special Care

Before putting your instrument back in its case after playing, do the following:

• Remove the reed and wipe off excess moisture. Return to reed case.

• Remove mouthpiece and wipe the inside with a clean cloth. Wash your mouthpiece once per week with warm tap water. Dry thoroughly.

• Remove the neck and shake out excess moisture. Dry with neck cleaner.

• Drop the weight of the chamois or cotton swab into the bell. Pull the swab through the body several times. Return the instrument to its case.

O = OPEN

● = PRESSED DOWN

The most common fingering appears first when two fingerings are shown.

Instrument courtesy of Yamaha Corporation of America Band and Orchestral Division.

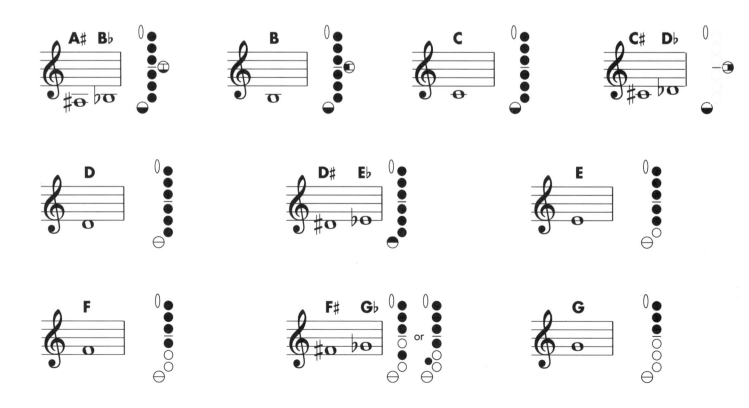

E♭ BARITONE SAXOPHONE FINGERING CHART

Take Special Care

Before putting your instrument back in its case after playing, do the following:

- Remove the reed and wipe off excess moisture. Return to reed case.
- Remove mouthpiece and wipe the inside with a clean cloth. Wash your mouthpiece once per week with warm tap water. Dry thoroughly.
- Remove the neck and shake out excess moisture. Dry with neck cleaner.
- Drop the weight of the chamois or cotton swab into the bell. Pull the swab through the body several times. Return the instrument to its case.

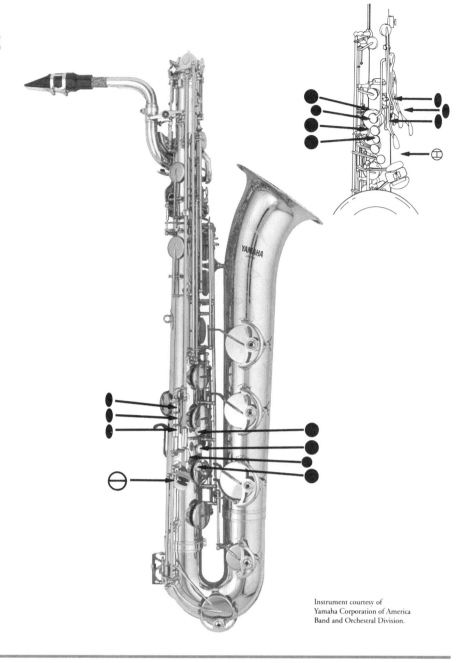

⭘ = OPEN

⬤ = PRESSED DOWN

The most common fingering appears first when two fingerings are shown.

Instrument courtesy of
Yamaha Corporation of America
Band and Orchestral Division.

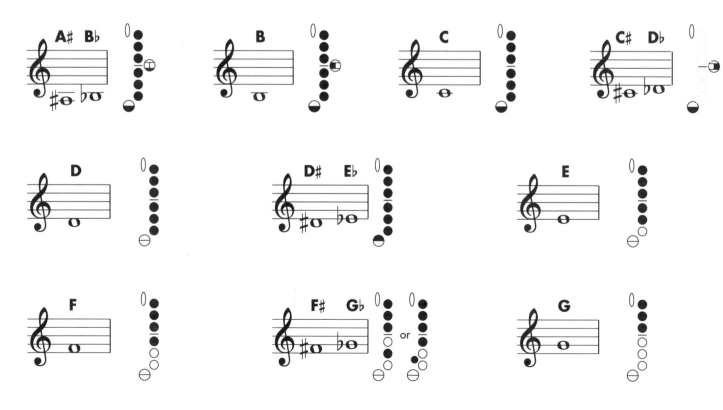

Bb TRUMPET/Bb CORNET FINGERING CHART

Bb Trumpet

Bb Cornet

 = UP    = PRESSED DOWN

Instruments courtesy of
Yamaha Corporation of America
Band and Orchestral Division.

Take Special Care

Before putting your instrument back in its case after playing, do the following:
- Use the water key to empty water from the instrument. Blow air through it..
- Remove the mouthpiece. Wash your mouthpiece with warm tap water once per week. Dry thoroughly.
- Wipe the instrument off with a clean soft cloth. Return the instrument to its case.

Trumpet valves occasionally need oiling. To oil your trumpet valves, simply:
- Unscrew the valve at the top of the casing.
- Lift the valve half-way out of the casing.
- Apply a few drops of oil to the exposed valve.
- Carefully return the valve to the casing. When properly inserted, the top of the valve should screw back into place.
- Be sure to grease the slides regularly. Your director will recommend valve oil and slide grease, and will help you apply them when necessary.

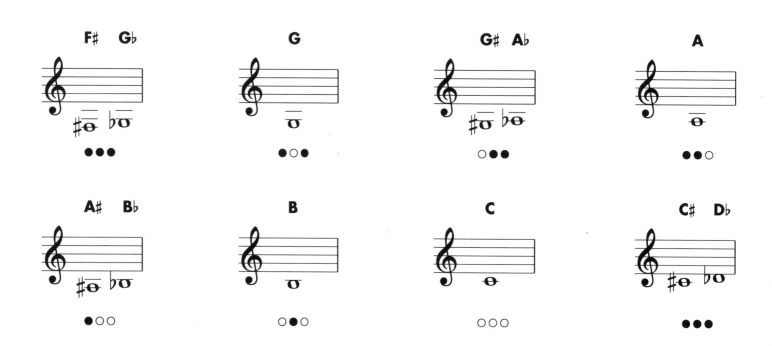

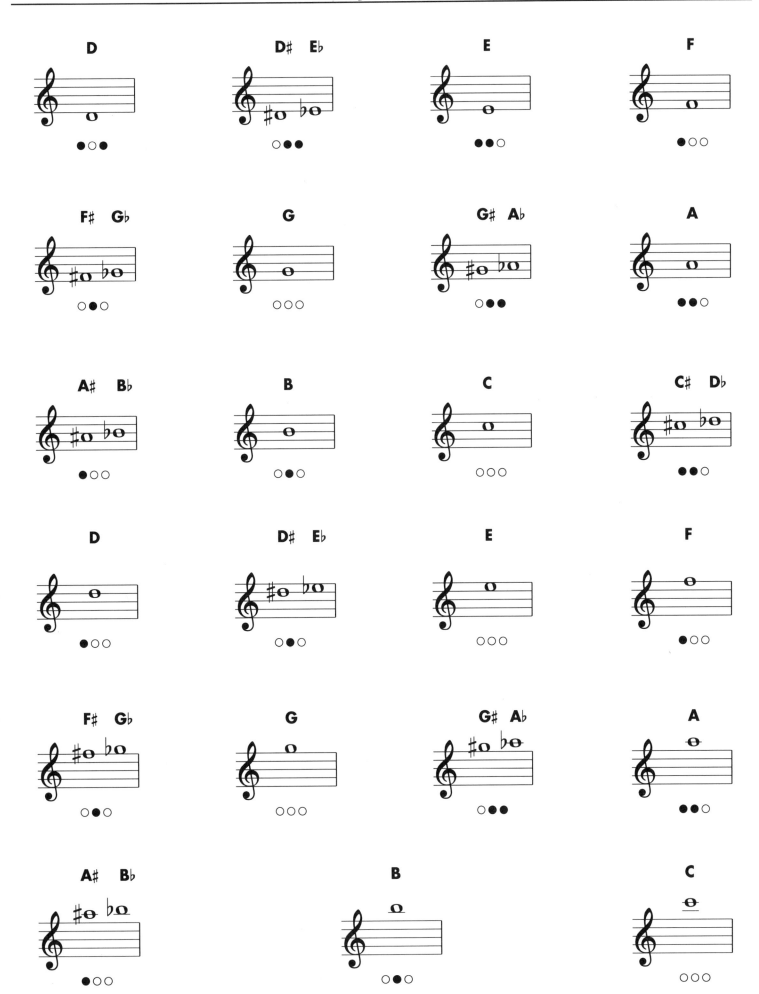

F HORN FINGERING CHART

 = UP

● = PRESSED DOWN

Take Special Care

Before putting your instrument back in its case after playing, do the following:

- Use the water key to empty water from the instrument. Blow air through it. If your horn does not have a water key, invert the instrument. You may also remove the main tuning slide, invert the instrument and remove excess water.
- Wipe the instrument off with a clean soft cloth. Return the instrument to its case.
- Remove the mouthpiece. Wash your mouthpiece with warm tap water once per week and dry thoroughly. Horn valves and slides occasionally need lubricating. Your director will recommend valve oil and slide grease, and will help you apply them when necessary.

F Horn players:
- Use the upper fingerings.

Double Horn players:
- Use the lower "T" fingerings when indicated. It is easier to play notes in the upper and extreme lower register of the horn using these fingerings.

B♭ Horn players:
- Use the lower fingerings. The "T" key is only used on double horns.

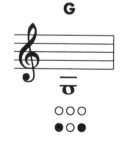

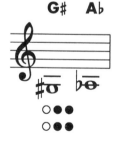

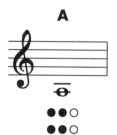

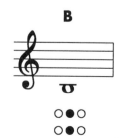

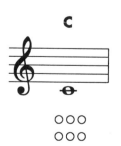

TROMBONE POSITION CHART

Numbers below the notes = Slide positions

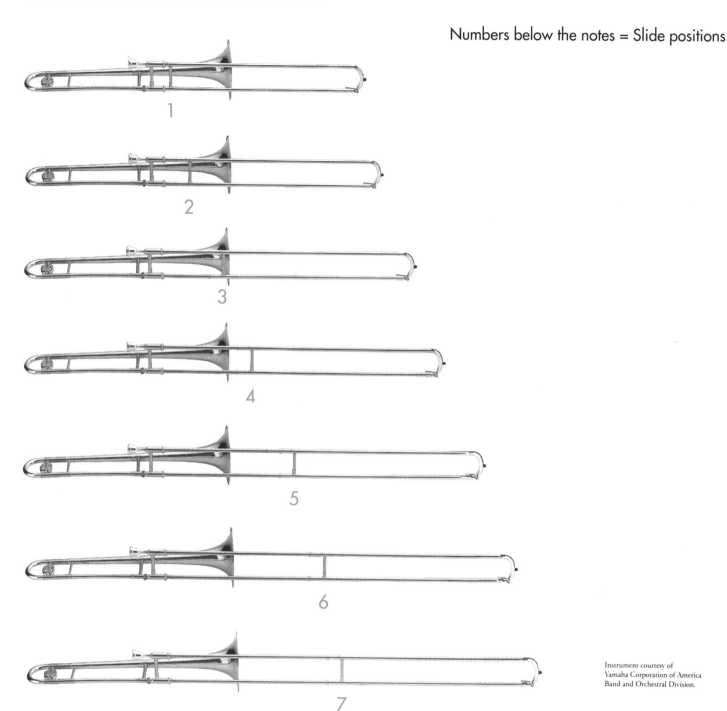

Instrument courtesy of
Yamaha Corporation of America
Band and Orchestral Division.

Take Special Care

Before putting your instrument back in its case after playing, do the following:
• Use the water key to empty water from the instrument. Blow air through it.
• Remove the mouthpiece and slide assembly. Do not take the outer slide off of the inner slide piece. Return the instrument to its case.
• Wash your mouthpiece with warm tap water once each week. Dry thoroughly.

Trombone slides occasionally need oiling. To oil your slide, simply:
• Rest the tip of the slide on the floor and unlock the slide.
• Exposing the inner slide, put a few drops of oil on the inner slide.
• Rapidly move the slide back and forth. The oil will then lubricate the slide.
• Be sure to grease the tuning slide regularly. Your director will recommend slide oil and grease, and will help you apply them when necessary.

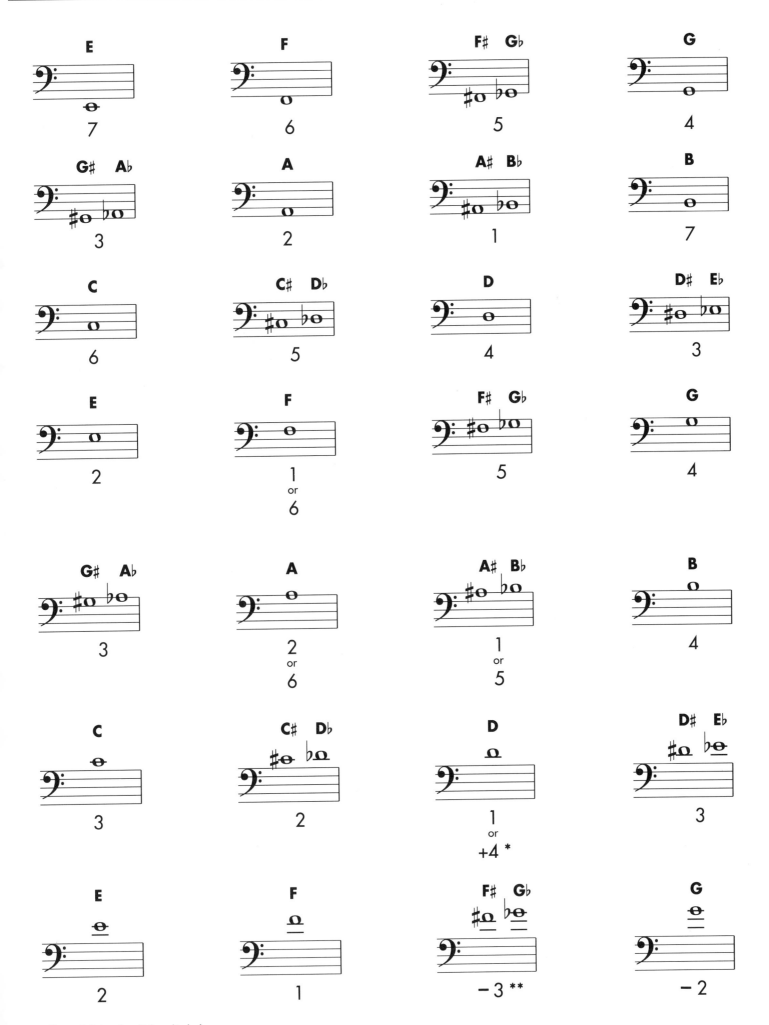

* **+** = Make the slide a little longer.
** **—** = Make the slide a little shorter.

BARITONE B.C. FINGERING CHART

Take Special Care

Before putting your instrument back in its case after playing, do the following:

- Use the water key to empty water from the instrument. Blow air through it.
- Remove the mouthpiece. Wash your mouthpiece with warm tap water once each week and dry thoroughly. Return the instrument to its case.

Baritone valves occasionally need oiling. To oil your valves, simply:

- Unscrew the valve at the top of the casing.
- Lift the valve half-way out of the casing.
- Apply a few drops of oil to the exposed metal valve.
- Carefully return the valve to the casing. When properly inserted, the top of the valve should screw back into place.
- Be sure to grease the slides regularly. Your director will recommend valve oil and slide grease, and will help you apply them when necessary.

○ = UP

● = PRESSED DOWN

Instrument courtesy of
Yamaha Corporation of America
Band and Orchestral Division.

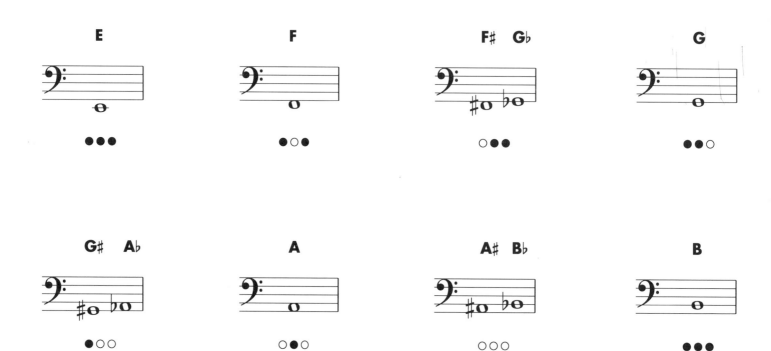

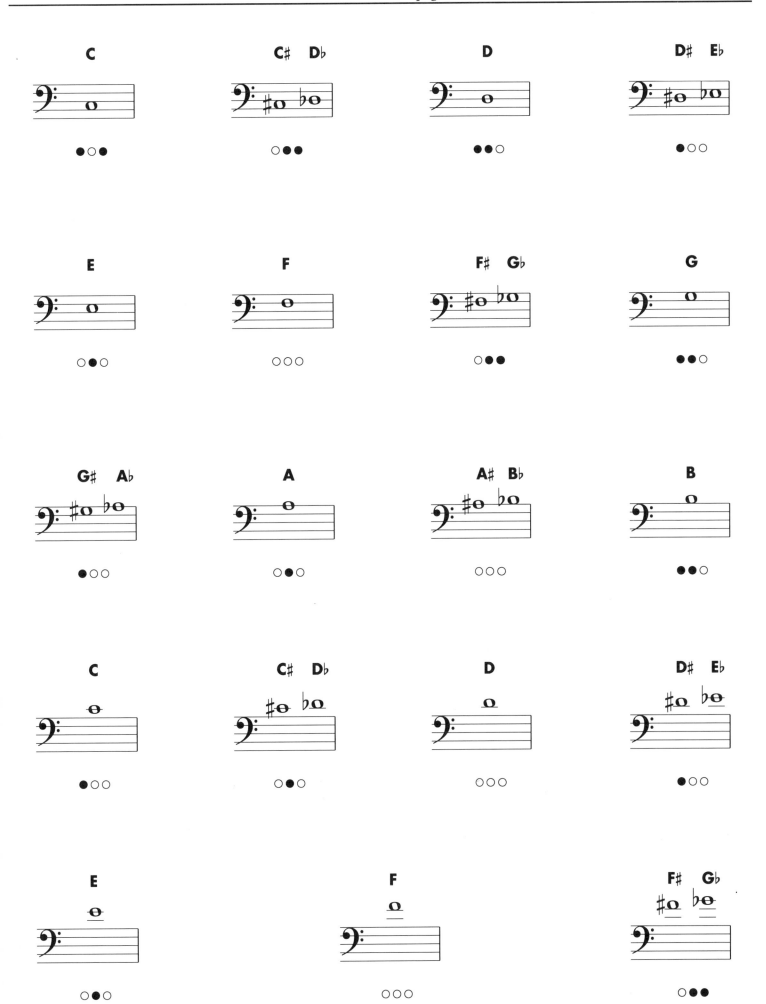

BARITONE T.C. FINGERING CHART

Take Special Care

Before putting your instrument back in its case after playing, do the following:

• Use the water key to empty water from the instrument. Blow air through it.

• Remove the mouthpiece. Wash your mouthpiece with warm tap water once each week and dry thoroughly. Return the instrument to its case.

Baritone valves occasionally need oiling. To oil your valves, simply:

• Unscrew the valve at the top of the casing.

• Lift the valve half-way out of the casing.

• Apply a few drops of oil to the exposed metal valve.

• Carefully return the valve to the casing. When properly inserted, the top of the valve should screw back into place.

• Be sure to grease the slides regularly. Your director will recommend valve oil and slide grease, and will help you apply them when necessary.

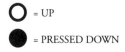

O = UP

● = PRESSED DOWN

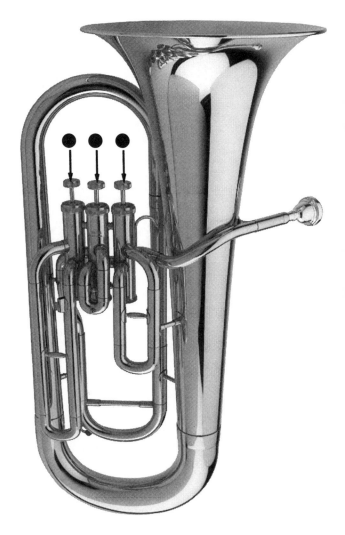

Instrument courtesy of
Yamaha Corporation of America
Band and Orchestral Division.

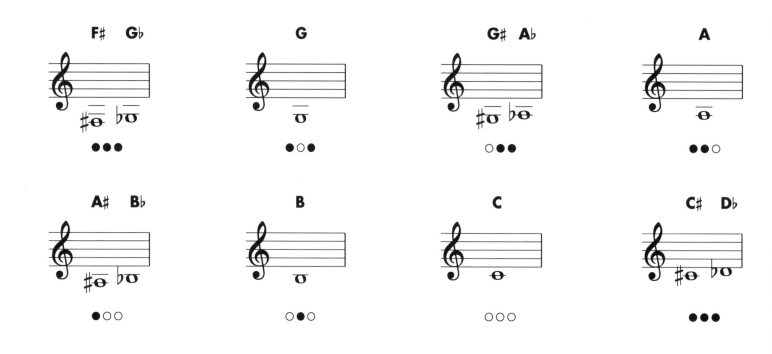

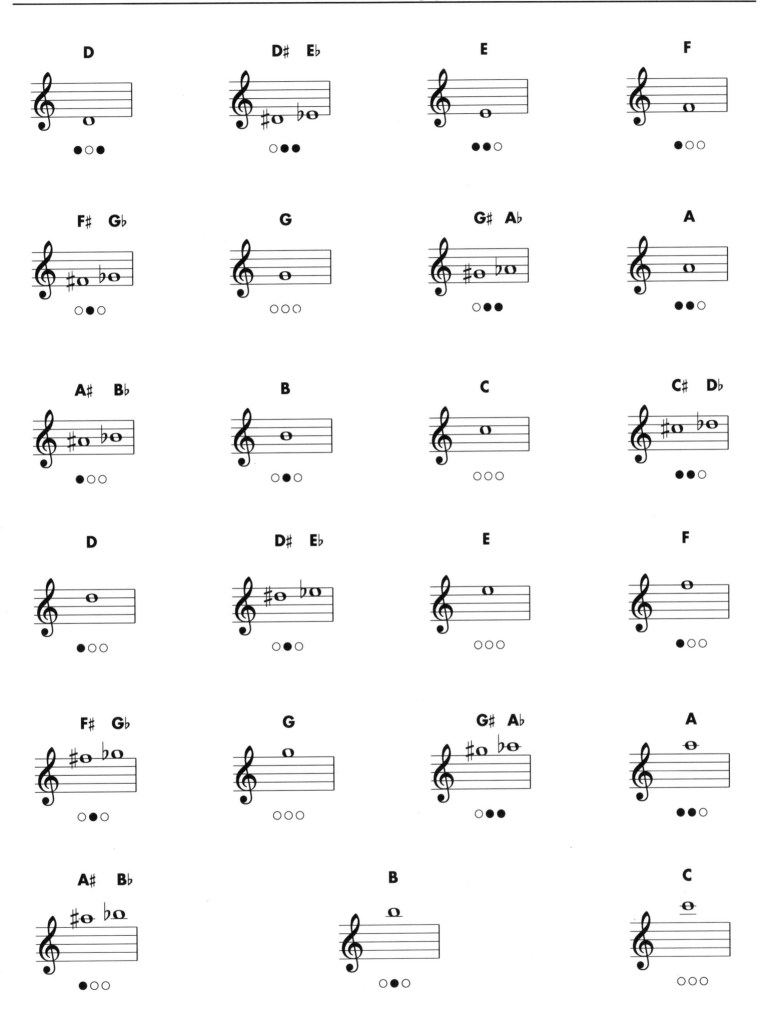

TUBA FINGERING CHART

Take Special Care

Before putting your instrument back in its case after playing, do the following:

• Use the water key to empty water from the instrument. Blow air through it.

• Remove the mouthpiece. Wash your mouthpiece with warm tap water once each week and dry thoroughly. Return the instrument to its case.

Tuba valves occasionally need oiling. To oil your valves, simply:

• Unscrew the valve at the top of the casing.

• Lift the valve half-way out of the casing.

• Apply a few drops of oil to the exposed metal valve.

• Carefully return the valve to the casing. When properly inserted, the top of the valve should screw back into place.

• Be sure to grease the slides regularly. Your director will recommend valve oil and slide grease, and will help you apply them when necessary.

$\bigcirc$ = UP

● = PRESSED DOWN

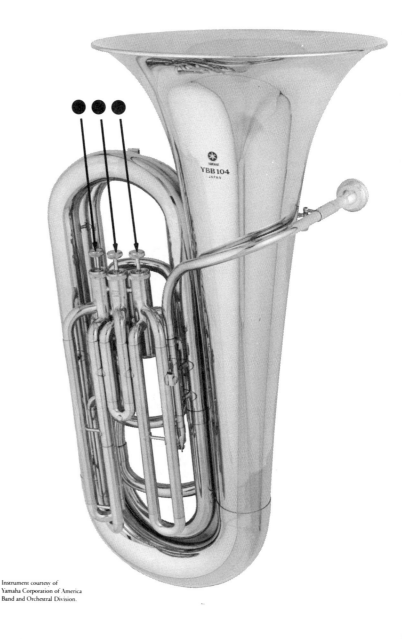

Instrument courtesy of
Yamaha Corporation of America
Band and Orchestral Division.

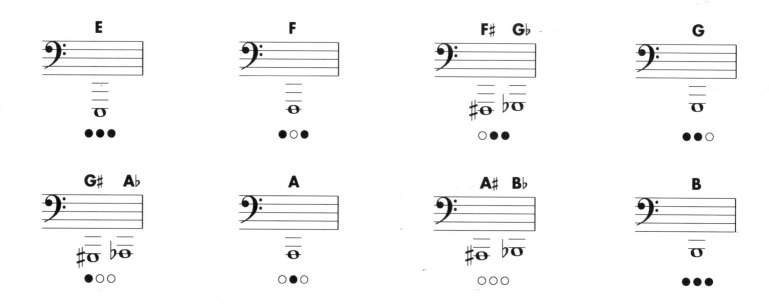

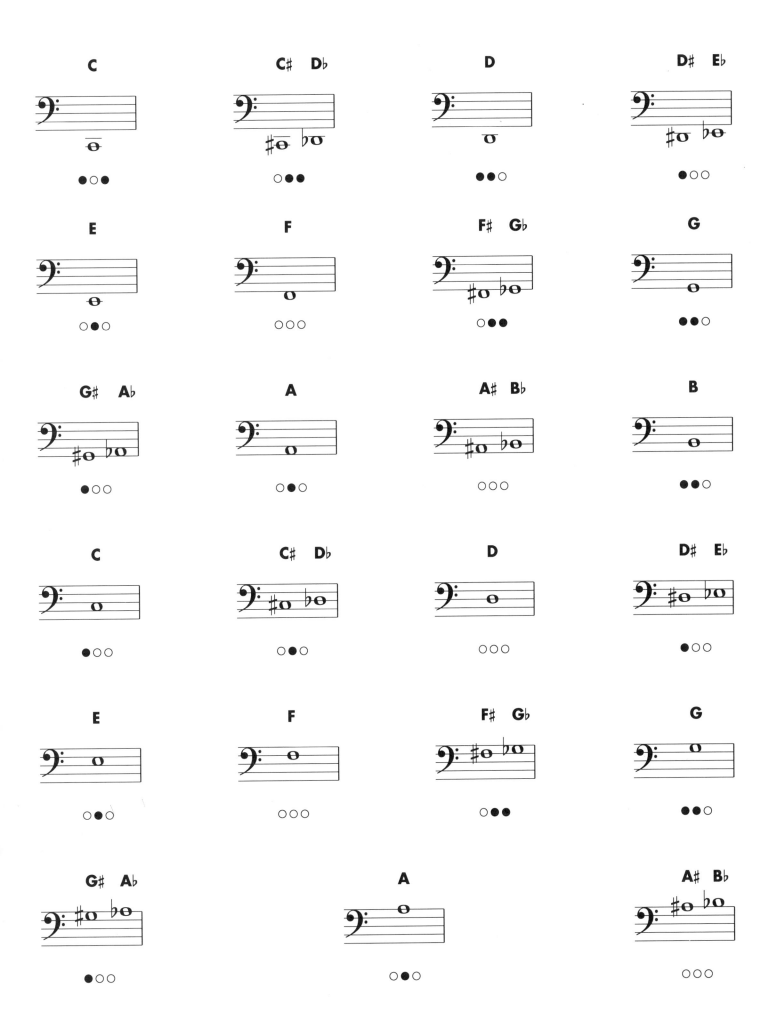

BASIC PERCUSSION EXERCISES

DYNAMIC STICKING CONTROL

Practice these exercises during your daily warm-up. Begin with slow tempos and gradually increase your speed. Play crescendos and decrescendos smoothly and evenly.

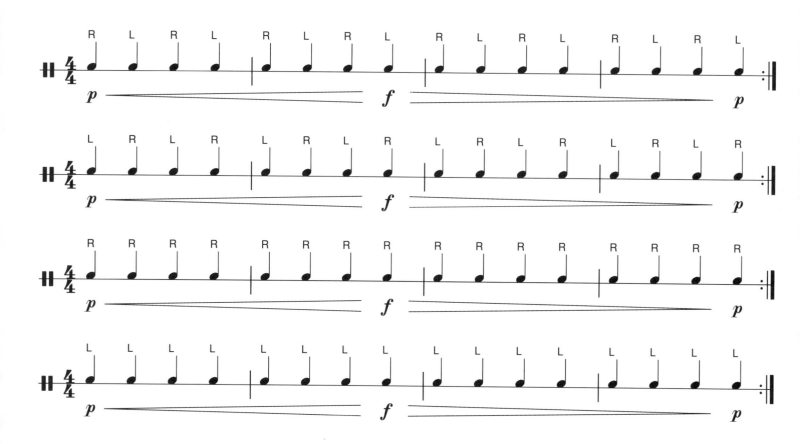

ROLLS WITHOUT RELEASE NOTES

You will often find rolls that are not connected to a release note. When you see this, simply roll for the full value of the note and lift both hands off the drum at the end of the count:

When non-release rolls follow each other, put a very slight separation between them. Lift the sticks and start the next roll on time:

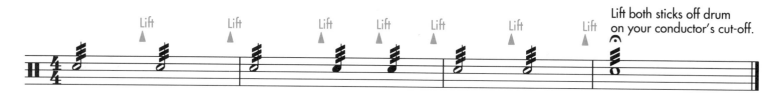

Percussionists must always listen and make their parts "fit" what is happening in the band at the same time. Play smooth and connected rolls when the band plays *legato*. Separate rolls during *marcato*, or accented sections. When in doubt, ask your conductor.

SNARE DRUM INTERNATIONAL DRUM RUDIMENTS

All rudiments should be practiced: open (slow) to close (fast) and/or at an even moderate march tempo.

Take Special Care

Snare drums occasionally need tuning. Ask your teacher to help you tighten each tension rod equally using a drum key.

- Be careful not to over-tighten the head. It will break if the tension is too tight.
- Loosen the snare strainer at the end of each rehearsal.
- Cover all percussion instruments when not in use.
- Put sticks away in a storage area. Keep the percussion section neat!
- Sticks are the only things which should be placed on the snare drum. NEVER put or allow others to put objects on any percussion instrument.

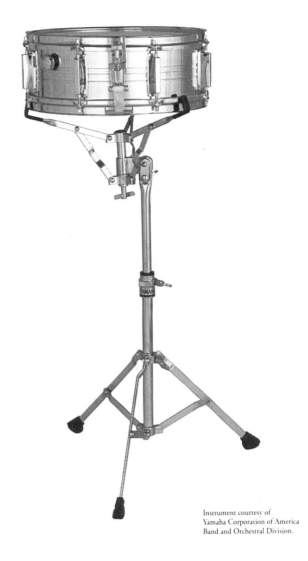

Instrument courtesy of
Yamaha Corporation of America
Band and Orchestral Division.

I. ROLL RUDIMENTS

A. SINGLE STROKE ROLL RUDIMENTS

1. Single Stroke Roll

R L R L R L R L

2. Single Stroke Four

R L R L R L R L
L R L R L R L R

3. Single Stroke Seven

R L R L R L R
L R L R L R L

B. MULTIPLE BOUNCE ROLL RUDIMENTS

4. Multiple Bounce Roll

5. Triple Stroke Roll

C. DOUBLE STROKE OPEN ROLL RUDIMENTS

6. Double Stroke Open Roll

11. Ten Stroke Roll
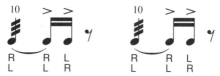

7. Five Stroke Roll

12. Eleven Stroke Roll
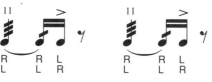

8. Six Stroke Roll
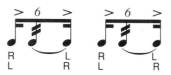

13. Thirteen Stroke Roll
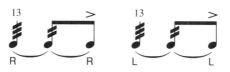

9. Seven Stroke Roll
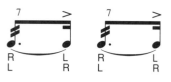

14. Fifteen Stroke Roll
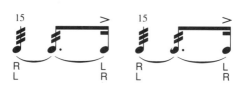

10. Nine Stroke Roll

15. Seventeen Stroke Roll

II. DIDDLE RUDIMENTS

16. Single Paradiddle

18. Triple Paradiddle

17. Double Paradiddle

19. Single Paradiddle-Diddle

III. FLAM RUDIMENTS

20. Flam

L R   R L

21. Flam Accent

L R L R   R L R L

22. Flam Tap

L R R R L L   L R R R L L

23. Flamacue

L R L R L   L R

24. Flam Paradiddle

L R L R R   R L R L L

25. Single Flammed Mill

L R R L R   R L L R L

26. Flam Paradiddle-Diddle

L R L R R L L   R L R L L R R

27. Pataflafla

L R L R R L   L R L R R L

28. Swiss Army Triplet

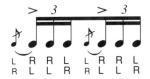

L R R L   L R R L
R L L R   R L L R

29. Inverted Flam Tap

L R L R L R   L R L R L R

30. Flam Drag

L R L L R   R L R R L

IV. DRAG RUDIMENTS

31. Drag

L L R   R R L

32. Single Drag Tap

L L R   L   R R L   R

33. Double Drag Tap

L L R L L R   L   R R L R R L   R

34. Lesson 25

L L R   L   R   L L R   L   R
R R L   R   L   R R L   R   L

35. Single Dragadiddle

R R L R   R   L L R L   L

36. Drag Paradiddle #1

R L L R L R R   L R R L R L L

37. Drag Paradiddle #2

R L L R L L R L R R   L R R L R R L R L L

38. Single Ratamacue

L L R L R L   R R L R L R

39. Double Ratamacue

L L R L L R L R L   R R R R L R L R

40. Triple Ratamacue

L L R L L R   L L R L R L   R R L R R L   R R L R L R

Director | This Keyboard Percussion instrument guide also appears in the Percussion book after the 40 International Drum Rudiments pages.

KEYBOARD PERCUSSION INSTRUMENTS

Each keyboard percussion instrument has a unique sound because of the materials used to create the instrument. Ranges may differ with some models of instruments.

Take Special Care
• Cover all percussion instruments when they are not being used.
• Put mallets away in a storage area. Keep the percussion section neat!
• Mallets are the only things which should be placed on your instrument. NEVER put or allow others to put objects on any percussion instrument.

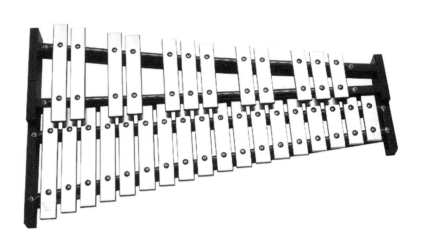

BELLS (Orchestra Bells)
• Bars - metal alloy or steel
• Mallets - lexan (hard plastic), brass or hard rubber
• Range - 2 1/2 octaves
• Sounds 2 octaves higher than written

XYLOPHONE
• Bars - wooden or synthetic
• Mallets- hard rubber
• Range - 3 octaves
• Sounds 1 octave higher than written

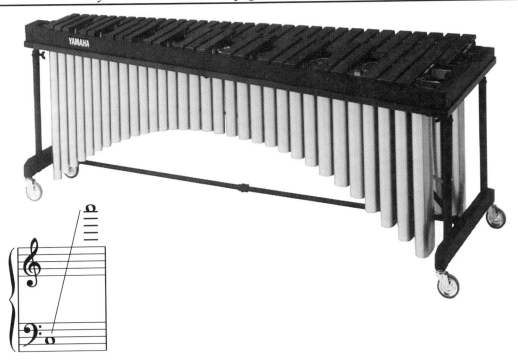

MARIMBA

- Bars - wooden (wider than xylophone bars) Resonating tube located below each bar
- Mallets - soft to medium rubber or yarn covered
- Range - 4 1/2 octaves (reads bass and treble clefs)
- Sounding pitch is the same as written pitch

VIBRAPHONE

- Bars - metal alloy or aluminum Resonating tubes located below each bar Adjustable electric fans in each resonator create "vibrato" effect
- Mallets - yarn covered
- Range - 3 octaves
- Sounding pitch is the same as written pitch

CHIMES

- Bars - metal tubes
- Mallets - plastic, rawhide or wooden
- Range - 1 1/2 octaves
- Sounding pitch is the same as written pitch

Instruments and photos courtesy of
Yamaha Corporation of America
Band and Orchestral Division.

GLOSSARY

Essential Element	Definition
Accelerando *accel.*	Gradually increase the tempo.
Accent	Emphasize the note.
Accidentals	Sharps, flats, and naturals found in the music.
Adagio	Slow tempo, slower than *Andante.*
Alla Breve	Another name for cut time.
Allegretto	A lively tempo.
Allegro	Fast bright tempo.
Andante	Slow walking tempo.
Arpeggio	A sequence of notes from any scale.
Balance	The proper adjustment of volume from all instruments.
Bar Lines	Divide the music staff into measures.
Bass Clef	"F" clef used by trbs., bar, bsn. and tuba.
Bizet, Georges	French composer (1838-1875).
Breath Mark	Take a deep breath after playing the note full value.
Chromatics	Notes that are altered with sharps, flats and naturals.
Chromatic Scale	Sequence of notes in half-steps.
Cohan, George M.	American composer (1878-1942).
Common Time	Another way to write $\frac{4}{4}$.
Crescendo	Gradually increase volume
Cut Time	Meter in which the half note gets one beat.
D.C. al Fine	*Da Capo al Fine* - Play until *D.C. al Fine.* Go back to the beginning and play until *Fine.*
D.S. al Fine	*Del Segno al Fine* - Play until *D.S. al Fine.* Go back to the sign (𝄋) and play until *Fine.*
Decrescendo	Gradually decrease volume.
Dotted Note	The dot adds half the value of the note.
Double Bar	Indicates the end of a piece of music.
Duet	Composition for two players.
Dynamics	The volume of music.
Edgar, Sir Edward	English composer (1857-1934).
Enharmonics	Notes that are written differently but sound the same.
Etude	A "study piece" for a technique.
Fermata	Hold the note longer, or until your director tells you to release it.
1st and 2nd Endings	Play the 1st ending the 1st time through. Then, repeat the same music, skip the 1st ending and play the 2nd.
Flat ♭	Lowers the note and remains in effect the entire measure.
forte *f*	Play loudly.
Gliére, Reinhold	Russian composer (1875-1956).
Habañera	Dance in slow $\frac{2}{4}$ meter.
Half-step	The smallest distance between two notes.
Interval	The numerical distance between two notes.
Key Signature	Flats or sharps next to the clef that apply to entire piece.

Essential Element	Definition
Legato	Play in a smooth and connected style.
Leger Lines	Adds notes outside of the music staff.
Maestoso	Play in a majestic, stately manner.
Major Scale	Series of 8 notes with a definite pattern of whole steps and half steps.
Measure	A segment of music divided by bar lines.
Measure Repeat	Repeat the previous measure.
mezzo forte *mf*	Play moderately loud.
mezzo piano *mp*	Play moderately soft.
Moderato	Moderate tempo.
Multiple Measures Rest	The number indicates how many measures to count and rest.
Music Staff	Lines and spaces where notes are placed.
Natural Sign ♮	Cancels a flat ♭ or sharp ♯ in the measure.
piano *p*	Play softly.
Pick-up Notes	Note or notes that come before the first full measure.
Rallentando *rall.*	Gradually slow the tempo.
Rehearsal Numbers	Measure numbers in squares above the staff.
Repeat Sign	Go back to the beginning and play again.
	Repeat the section of music enclosed by repeat signs.
Rests	Silent beats of music.
Ritardando *rit.*	Gradually slow the tempo.
Round or Canon	Musical form where instruments play the same melody entering at different times.
Sharp ♯	Raises the note and remains in effect the entire measure.
Sightreading	Playing a musical selection for the first time.
Simile *sim.*	Continue in the same style.
Slur	A curved line that connects notes of different pitches.
Sousa, John Philip	American composer (1854-1932).
Staccato	Play the notes with separation.
Strauss, Johann	Austrian composer (1825-1899).
Syncopation	Accents on the weak beats of the music.
Tallis, Thomas	English composer (1505-1585).
Tempo	The speed of music.
Tenuto	Play notes for their full value.
Tie	A curved line that connects notes of the same pitch.
Time Signature (Meter)	Tells how many beats are in each measure and what kind of note gets one beat.
Treble Clef	"G" clef used by fls., ob., clar., sax. and tpt.
Trio	Composition for three players.
Triplet	Group of three notes.
Waltz	Dance in moderate $\frac{3}{4}$ meter.

HISTORY OF THE BAND

Beginning To Present Day

Our present-day concert band is a close cousin of the early military bands and the adaptation of concert literature to the brass, woodwind, and percussion sections of the symphony orchestra. Having become an entity of its own in this century, the concert band has become the fundamental ensemble of the whole band idiom which includes: jazz band, marching band, woodwind, brass, and percussion ensembles, and a host of other tailored groups from Dixieland bands to pit groups for musicals.

After a town parade, it was customary for the featured band to wind up at the community park and play a concert of musical favorites for the patrons. Much of the early literature featured transcriptions of orchestral favorites demanding the woodwinds to replace the symphony string sections. The programs were embellished with the traditional and popular marches and folk songs of the day and this musical event became a custom passed on from one generation to the next. Various techniques and skills were traded "on the bandstand" and as children grew up, the family instrument was carefully handed to the next aspiring musician with hopes of continued enjoyment of being a part of the band.

In the early part of the 20th century, the school bands began to appear. Performing at various school and community functions, this organization quickly took on the identity of the local school and became a flagship for the area people. Teachers who were skilled in some facet of music began to work with beginning classes and we soon had the formalized structure of the band programs as we know them today. Instrument manufacturers worked hand-in-hand with administrators to create sound curriculums. The popularity of the traveling bands, Sousa, Goldman, etc., was enjoying national acclaim and the band movement across America became an established and welcome part of our schools and our lives.

With this new medium of expression available, composers turned their attention and artistic pens in the direction of the band instrumentation. Internationally, composers came to the forefront and wrote specifically for the tonal texture of the band. As a result, we enjoy an ever-growing library of creative styles written for all levels of musical proficiency from the beginner to the professional performer.

Today almost every school in our nation offers band as a part of the school day agenda. Many young people seek a career in the world of music. Colleges offer degrees in music performance, music education, music composition, music recording, music industry, and a host of other music related professions. Many adults in other professions are now spending their free time playing in local community bands which are flourishing throughout the country.

BAND IS A LIFETIME EXPERIENCE. The musician in every human longs to be heard and band offers the opportunity to all artists who have a message to share.

CAREERS IN MUSIC

Director   The real benefits of being involved in music are the life long skills of self-discipline, team work, goal setting, self-expression, problem solving, self-confidence, concentration and much more.

The following outline and activities provide students with the opportunity of learning about the diverse careers in music. By discussing these topics, you may increase the possibility that your students will become patrons of the arts, regardless of their chosen career. Present these career options to the class and encourage discussion.

MUSIC EDUCATION
• Band Director
• Orchestra Director
• Choir Director
• Elementary Music Specialist
• Private Studio Instructor (Instrumental, Piano, Voice)
• College Professor (Instrumental, Piano, Voice, History, Theory, Conducting)

Activity
• You are the band director role model for your class. Discuss your decision to be a band director. Invite another music teacher from your district or university to present a brief presentation for the class.

MUSIC THERAPY
•Music Therapist

Activity
• Invite a music therapist to present music therapy techniques to your class. You may also be able to attend a music therapy concert or recital in your area.

MUSIC MERCHANDISING
• Sheet Music Dealers
• Instrument Dealers
• Record/CD Dealers

Activity
• Arrange to take a field trip to a local sheet music, instrument or record store.

MUSIC MANUFACTURING
• Musical Instruments
• Recording/Electronic Equipment
• Record/CD Manufacturing

Activity
• Invite an instrument manufacturer's representative to your class to discuss the techniques used when making various band and orchestral instruments.

COMPOSITION
- Band, Orchestral and Choral Composer/Arranger
- Movie Soundtracks/Background Music Composer
- TV Commercial Jingles Writer
- Pop Music Writer

Activity
- Ask students to name famous composers from **Essential Elements Book 1** and **Book 2**. Invite a composer-in-residence from your area to speak to the class about the importance of learning the essential elements of music. Ask your students to compose a solo for their instrument and perform it for the class.

CONDUCTING
- Concert/Symphonic/Community Band Conductor
- Symphony/Chamber/Community Orchestra Conductor

Activity
- When the local high school band invites a guest conductor/clinician, arrange a field trip to watch the rehearsal and concert.

MUSIC/SOUND PRODUCTION
- Recording Studio Engineer
- Record Producer

Activity
- Visit a local recording studio, or watch a video of how records/CD's are produced.

MUSIC PERFORMANCE
- Studio Musician
- Professional Ensemble Player
- Symphony Orchestra Musician
- Opera Singer
- Jazz/Blues/Rock/Pop Singer
- Rock Band Musician

Activity
- Invite a professional musician from your area to speak to the class about their work.

MUSIC PUBLISHING
- Music Editor
- Engraver
- Graphic Artist
- Typesetter
- Sales Person

Activity
- Stop at a music publisher's exhibit while attending your next state or national convention. Ask the publisher about their work, and discuss it with your students.

PROGRAMMING IDEAS

It's concert time! Young musicians await this moment with eager anticipation which can be focused to support the continued growth and development of the individual musician and the program. As the *director* you can create a stage of acknowledgement and appreciation for students, parents, and all those in the audience via wise programming. Here are some *positive pogramming tips* which can serve as guidelines in this most important endeavor.

Red Letter Date

As soon as the concert date is set, begin to send notices home, alert the media, and remind the students at every rehearsal. To ensure a successful concert experience, it is imperative that you have a representative audience to support the performers. You may want to seek a volunteer parent to organize a phone campaign of personal invitations to the families of the young musicians. Use every communication vehicle at your disposal to make certain the community is aware of this important musical presentation.

Pre-Performance Education

It is always advantageous to send home a reminder of *concert etiquette*. It is also important to spend part of band class discussing the appropriate manners and deportment expected of the musicians as well as the audience. Tastefully remind the audience of their need to be appreciative, focused on the concert, and enthusiastic in their support of the performers. It is an opportunity to enroll the parents and students in a joint learning process and establish positive standards for the future.

Musical Variety

As with any production, the program must have something for everyone. Full band pieces can be exchanged with feature ensembles, soloists, student conductors, etc. Consider using one of the high school musicians as a soloist or a neighboring director as a guest artist or conductor. Perhaps you might want to bring in one of the older groups for a cameo appearance; i.e., high school percussion ensemble, clarinet quartet, etc. Program stylistic changes which will appeal to different facets of the audience such as overtures, ballads, Latin selections, and marches.

Communicate With The Audience

The concert offers a perfect opportunity to create a stage of familiarity and understanding. This is not only a chance to affirm the significance of the band, but also to explain the importance of artistic expression and garner their future support. Addressing the audience between each composition allows the musicians to make necessary adjustments, rest their embouchures, and adequately prepare for the next musical presentation. As a reward, certain students might be chosen to announce various selections and share pertinent program notes with the audience. The communication with the concert audience is part of the performance and should be aptly prepared and rehearsed with the same importance as the music.

Spotlight Of Due Praise

Everyone thrives on appreciation for a job well done. At the completion of each piece, appropriately spotlight those musicians who were featured. Once they are standing and have been acknowledged, ask the rest of the supporting ensemble to stand for their due credit.

If there is a particularly difficult part for one of the sections, this might be highlighted in the program notes or by the announcer/director. Inform the audience of special points of interest in the upcoming composition so they will understand the technique level the students have developed to accommodate the musical demands.

Included with the names of the performers, concert programs should offer *special thanks* to all the support cast of volunteers who have aided in the concert preparation and presentation. Recognition of those who aided will warrant their participation in future ventures.

An announced reminder to reinforce those on the concert program will guarantee a solid audience for the next event.

Involve Administration

Here is an occasion to invite an administrator to welcome the audience or extend some personal thoughts during the evening about the importance of *music education* in their child's life. Each concert might feature a different principal, board member, and so forth. It is important for everyone to see the support of the administrators and for them to take an active role in the program.

A Forum Of Exchange

Once the musical performance is completed, make yourself available for questions and comments. A reception in the school cafeteria might be in order which would promote exchange between parents and allow the students to enjoy the fruits of their labor. The inclusion of a volunteer parent group to organize this is another positive effort which benefits the program and affords a larger participation.

You Are The Key

It is the responsibility of the director to communicate with as many members of the audience as possible. Be assertive in your gracious thank yous and take time to introduce yourself to as many parents as possible. It is important they understand it is *their band*. They are the reason for the success of the program. The home practice program and the encouraging words of Mom and Dad are the foundations of any successful band program. Nurture this with constant care and attention. There is never a more apropos time than following a great concert.

BIBLIOGRAPHY

Baker, Theodore. *The Concise Baker's Biographical Dictionary Of Musicians*. Edited by Nicolas Slonimsky. New York: Schirmer Books, 1988.

Barlow, Harold, and Sam Morgenstern, comps. *A Dictionary of Musical Themes*. rev. ed. New York: Crown Publishers, 1975.

Farkas, Philip. *The Art of French Horn Playing*. Secaucus, New Jersey: Summy-Birchard, 1956.

Grout, Donald J. *A History of Western Music*. rev. ed. New York: W.W. Norton & Company, 1988.

Holloway, Ronald A., and Harry R. Bartlett. *Guide to Teaching Percussion*. 4th ed. revised by John J. Papastefan. Dubuque, Iowa: William C. Brown Publishers, 1984.

Hunt, Norman J. *Guide to Teaching Brass*. 3rd ed. Dubuque, Iowa: William C. Brown Publishers, 1984.

Kleinhammer, Edward. *The Art of Trombone Playing*. Princeton, New Jersey: Summy-Birchard, 1963.

Peters, Gordon B. *The Drummer: Man: A Treatise on Percussion*. rev. ed. Wilmette, Illinois: Kemper Peters Publications, 1975.

Putnik, Edwin. *The Art of Flute Playing*. rev. ed. Secaucus, New Jersey: Summy-Birchard, 1970.

Sadie, Stanley, ed. *The New Grove Dictionary of Music and Musicians*. 20 vols. London: Macmillian Publishers, 1980.

Sadie, Stanley, and Alison Latham, eds. *The Norton/Grove Concise Encyclopedia of Music*. New York: W.W. Norton & Company, 1988.

Spencer, William. *The Art of Bassoon Playing*. Revised by Frederick Muller. Princeton, New Jersey: Summy-Birchard, 1958.

Sprenkle, Robert, and David Ledet. *The Art of Oboe Playing*. Secaucus, New Jersey: Summy-Birchard, 1961.

Stein, Keith. *The Art of Clarinet Playing*. Secaucus, New Jersey: Summy-Birchard, 1958.

Teal, Larry. *The Art of Saxophone Playing*. Secaucus, New Jersey: Summy-Birchard, 1963.

Westphal, Frederick W. *Guide to Teaching Woodwinds*. 5th ed. Dubuque, Iowa: William C. Brown Publishers, 1990.

*Special thanks to the editors, music engravers, typesetters and artists
of Hal Leonard Publishing Corporation who greatly assisted in the writing and design of this book.*

INSTRUMENTATION

Essential Elements Book 1

00863501	Flute
00863502	Oboe
00863503	Bassoon
00863504	B♭ Clarinet
00863505	E♭ Alto Clarinet
00863506	B♭ Bass Clarinet
00863507	E♭ Alto Saxophone
00863508	B♭ Tenor Saxophone
00863509	E♭ Baritone Saxophone
00863510	B♭ Trumpet
00863511	F Horn
00863512	Trombone
00863513	Baritone B.C.
00863514	Baritone T.C.
00863515	Tuba
00863516	Percussion
00863517	Keyboard Percussion
00863518	Conductor

00860100	Teacher Resource Kit

Essential Elements Book 2

00863519	Flute
00863520	Oboe
00863521	Bassoon
00863522	B♭ Clarinet
00863523	E♭ Alto Clarinet
00863524	B♭ Bass Clarinet
00863525	E♭ Alto Saxophone
00863526	B♭ Tenor Saxophone
00863527	E♭ Baritone Saxophone
00863528	B♭ Trumpet
00863529	F Horn
00863530	Trombone
00863531	Baritone B.C.
00863532	Baritone T.C.
00863533	Tuba
00863534	Percussion
00863535	Keyboard Percussion
00863536	Conductor

See your favorite band music dealer for the latest releases from these levels of the **Essential Elements Band Series:**

Explorer Level	Correlated with Book 1, page 7
Performer Level	Correlated with Book 1, page 17
Artist Level	Correlated with Book 1, page 29
Expert Level	Correlated with Book 2, page 14
Master Level	Correlated with Book 2, page 29